Other Hay House Lifestyles Titles of Related Interest

Books

Dr. Wayne Dyer's 10 Secrets for Success and Inner Peace
(available August 2002)
Healing with Herbs and Home Remedies A–Z, by Hanna Kroeger
Heal Your Body A–Z, by Louise L. Hay
Inner Wisdom, by Louise L. Hay
Interpreting Dreams A–Z, by Leon Nacson
The Love and Power Journal, by Lynn V. Andrews
Simple Things, by Jim Brickman
Space Clearing A–Z, by Denise Linn
What Color Is Your Personality?, by Carol Ritberger, Ph.D.
You Can Heal Your Life Gift Edition, by Louise L. Hay

Card Decks

Feng Shui Personal Paradise Cards (booklet and card deck),
by Terah Kathryn Collins
Healing with the Fairies Oracle Cards (booklet and card deck),
by Doreen Virtue, Ph.D.
Heart and Soul, by Sylvia Browne
MarsVenus Cards, by John Gray
Miracle Cards, by Marianne Williamson
Power Thought Cards, by Louise L. Hay
Self-Care Cards, by Cheryl Richardson
Wisdom Cards, by Louise L. Hay

All of the above titles are available through your local bookstore,
or may be ordered by calling Hay House at: (800) 654-5126

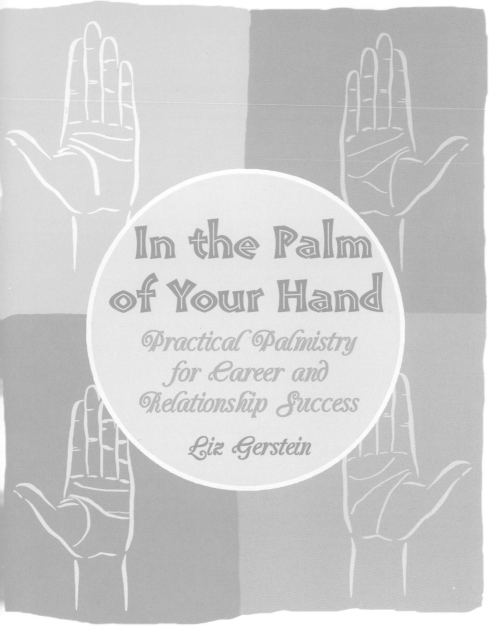

In the Palm of Your Hand

Practical Palmistry for Career and Relationship Success

Liz Gerstein

Hay House, Inc.
Carlsbad, California • Sydney, Australia
Canada • Hong Kong • United Kingdom

Published and distributed in the United States by:
    Hay House, Inc., P.O. Box 5100, Carlsbad, CA 92018-5100 •
(800) 654-5126 • (800) 650-5115 (fax) • www.hayhouse.com
    Hay House Australia Pty Ltd, P.O. Box 515, Brighton-Le-Sands NSW
2216 • *phone:* 1800 023 516 • *e-mail:* info@hayhouse.com.au

Editorial Supervision: Jill Kramer • *Cover Design:* Christy Salinas
Interior Design: Summer McStravick
Illustrations: Gayle Kabaker

Library of Congress Cataloging-in-Publication Data

Gerstein, Liz.
    In the palm of your hand : practical palmistry for career and
relationship success / Liz Gerstein.
        p. cm.
    Includes bibliographical references.
    ISBN 1-56170-810-0
    1. Palmistry. I. Title.

 BF921 .G39 2002
 133.6--dc21

                                                    2001051859

              ISBN 1-56170-810-0

        05 04 03 02   4 3 2 1
        1st printing, March 2002

        Printed in China by Imago

Contents

Part I: A Manual of Modern Scientific Palmistry

- General Information
- The Size of the Hands
- Thick and Thin Hands; Firm and Soft Hands
- Skin Texture
- The Handshake

Part II: The Lines and Markings on the Palmar Surface

Part III: Using Practical Palmistry to Discover Your Inborn Talents and Potential

Preface

*T*he word *palmistry* tends to elicit a patronizing smile or a shrug of the shoulders, for most people don't believe that the study of hands has any genuine scientific merit. But we humans have always tried to untangle the complicated interaction between our physical, emotional, and intellectual realms so that we may uncover our "true selves." This search for identity is clearly confirmed by the countless self-help books on psychology, astrology, numerology, face reading, and graphology (the study of handwriting) that are in bookstores today.

Speaking of graphology, I've been a handwriting analyst for more than 20 years—at first, it was just a hobby, but it later became a career. I'm particularly interested in assessing the body and mind connection of individuals. Our hands are simply tools for transmitting our thoughts to paper—hence, handwriting has been (and should be) called "brainwriting." Even people who don't have the use of their hands produce the same psychological, emotional, and intellectual profile by holding a pen between their toes or in their mouth.

My natural curiosity and belief that every part of our unique self is interrelated and forms a piece of the puzzle led me to study related sciences, such as phrenology, and in particular, palmistry. After all, our hands form a microcosm of our entire body (the macrocosm). The lines, creases, and markings etched upon the palmar surface are a result of the activities from our central nervous system, thereby forming a connection with our handwriting.

How did I get started learning about palmistry? I first went to some libraries, where many books on the subject were available. My most valuable sources, however, were used bookstores, where I found some out-of-print "old treasures." In my travels to Europe, I also collected French and German books on palmistry. Every book provided me with its own particular information, and I was able to verify and integrate this by studying many hands, starting with my own. Then came those of family members and friends, who were only too pleased to help in my research. The first opportunity to test my knowledge came when I was asked to read hands for a charity fund-raising event. My only request was that they call my service "palm reading" instead of "fortune telling"! I was gratified by the response to my hand analysis, as complete strangers verified much of what I told them about their abilities, interests, and oft-hidden talents. After that event, I felt the confidence to call myself a "palmist"!

One of my reasons for writing this book is to dispel the "voodoo magic" attached to palmistry. If taken seriously and holistically, hands can provide valuable insight into our personality and the state of our physical and emotional health. This knowledge will hopefully lead to self-development and a greater enjoyment of life.

In this book, I'll discuss the practical application of palmistry, which explains how you can discover your inborn career potential and talents; I'll then go on to list the factors of compatibility in relationships. I'm hoping that *In the Palm of Your Hand* will be a source of enjoyment, and that it will create sufficient interest in you, the reader, to embark on a truly fascinating adventure into the art and mystery of hands, for it's my aim to guide you toward realizing your greatest fulfillment . . . in *all* aspects of your life.

The Origins and History of Palmistry

*T*he origins of palmistry may be much older than we think. In fact, some anthropologists believe that some handprints found in pre-historic caves date back to the Stone Age and were used in religious initiation ceremonies.

Fingerprints have been called "the ancient key to identity." Two thousand years before Christianity, Babylonians put their fingerprints on soft clay to protect against the forgery of important documents. In ancient China, the impressions of fingerprints served as signatures by those unable to sign their name, and even the emperor resorted to using his thumbprint to sign important papers. Until 1860, the Japanese followed similar practices; they also put their fingerprints on the front doors of their homes for protection.

During Alexander the Great's reign (356–323 B.C.), the Hellenic civilization reached great heights in the arts and sciences. Aristotle, the philosopher who was Alexander's tutor, imparted much of his knowledge and interest in all methods of prophecy, such as astronomy, astrology, graphology, and chiromancy (the science of hand reading) to him.

It seems only fitting that the study of the hands should be called *chiromancy,* which is derived from the Greek word *cheir,* meaning "hand"; and *manteia,* meaning "divination." The name was later popularized as *palmistry,* which is derived from the Latin word *paume,* meaning "palm." This reveals that the studies pertaining to the anatomy of the hand and those of the linear patterns and creases etched into the palm and fingertips were treated as separate sciences, even hundreds of years ago.

Interest in the study of the hands was clearly portrayed by artists during the 16th and 17th centuries. However, when gypsies from Northern India swarmed over Europe, they brought with them a different kind of palmistry. Their aura of mysticism contributed to the fear and fascination people had for their predictions. Sadly, these prophecies often materialized through the power of positive or negative suggestions, which only strengthened people's fears, and belief in the gypsies' fortune- and misfortune-telling abilities. Eventually, the gypsies found their way to the Court of England; it was rumored that King Henry VIII was a staunch believer in palmistry.

Casimir Stanislas d'Arpentigny of France (1798–1865) was said to have received his first knowledge of palmistry from a gypsy. Obviously fascinated and intrigued, he went on to study the old masters of chiromancy and later developed his own methods of reading hands. A lasting contribution is his classification of the six basic (and one "mixed") hand types, a technique that's still being used today. Because of this new method, d'Arpentigny is considered by many to be the father of modern palmistry, a fame that is shared with another Frenchman, Adrien Adolphe Desbarolles (1801–1886).

British scholar Noel Jaquin was another person who made great strides in the practical application and development of palmistry. In the early 19th century, he produced a book titled *Scientific Palmistry*, which contained some very forward-thinking ideas. For instance, he wrote that "the main object of the study of the hand is the prevention of latent diseases and the prevention of wasted years of effort and energy spent following a career for which the individual is unfitted," thus pointing to his studies in the field of career selection, a subject that I will discuss later in this book.

The 20th century produced—and the 21st century continues to bring forth—modern scientists who advance our knowledge of chiromancy. For instance, Julius Spier of Switzerland focused his studies on children's hands, and his work greatly impressed pioneer psychologist Carl Jung.

Cheiro

One of history's most colorful and charismatic palm readers, authors, and lecturers was Count Louis Hamon (1866–1936), better known as "Cheiro," which translates from the Greek as "hand reader." Cheiro's services were sought out by royal circles, and in 1896, *The Language of the Hand* was published in England. It gained immense recognition and was subsequently reprinted 33 times in England and in the United States, and was translated into many languages.

Celebrities from all over the world—including Mark Twain, Douglas Fairbanks, Erich von Stroheim, and Oscar Wilde—also wanted Cheiro to read their palms. Speaking of Wilde, in his book *Cheiro's Complete Palmistry,* Cheiro recounts an anecdote that took place during one of his fashionable parlor games in London. Cheiro would analyze anonymous hands that had been extended to him through a curtain without being able to see to whom they belonged.

As Wilde's hands were presented to him, Cheiro exclaimed in astonishment: "The left hand is that of a king, but the right one is that of a king who will send himself into exile." Wilde left the party without saying a word, for at that time he was the toast of London, having just produced his popular play *A Woman of No Importance.* But few people were aware of Wilde's decadence and debauchery, which later were made public during a sensational trial where Wilde was accused and convicted of sexual perversion and corruption. He was sent to prison and later exiled to France, where he died penniless and was shunned by his former influential friends. I'm guessing that Cheiro must have seen brilliance and success in

Wilde's left hand (his birth hand), while his right, or dominant, hand probably revealed a negative development of his character that included self-indulgence and a lack of morals. Unfortunately, Cheiro didn't specify or explain the signs and markings in Wilde's right hand upon which he based his analysis.

The Many Uses of Palmistry

As man is a microcosm of the macrocosm, the hand is a microcosm of our physical and mental entity, and is therefore a reflection of our personality. As Noel Jaquin said: "Success or failure is to be found in the combination of health and character."

An infant is born with its own blueprint of inherent characteristics, some of which are also indicated by the shape and structure of the hands, as well as in the lines, creases, and other markings imprinted upon the palmar surface and fingers. Some of the lines are subject to change through later development, while others, such as the patterns of the capillary ridges on fingertips, are permanently engraved. Being totally unique, they serve as a means of identification, as already mentioned.

The scholars studying hands realized early on, at least since the time of the Renaissance, that lines don't appear by accident and aren't merely the result of repetitive folding or flexing of the hands. Each line and additional marking has a special significance and must first be interpreted separately, then evaluated and balanced against other findings. Thus, with the myriad of differences in lines and markings, it makes each hand truly unique, so unique that even the left and right hands of a person aren't exactly alike.

Experiences from early childhood through the later stages of development combine with inherited tendencies, which are in our DNA and are factors in the formation of the personality. Behaviorists and geneticists will always be divided as to whether inherited characteristics or the influence of the environment is more significant. Says Harvard sociobiologist E. O. Wilson: "Nature determines how the individual responds to nurture."

In the case of children and young adults, discovering potential strengths and weaknesses would be valuable and significant, as dormant mental powers and talents can be cultivated. But if one is aware of negative traits or tendencies, they may be eliminated or corrected by proper training and diets, relating to the physical health of an individual.

It's easy to see why and how the study of the hand could be valuable in the selection of a career. As an example, hands that are square and broad in shape indicate inborn practical tendencies, and if these characteristics are coupled with sturdy fingers, such a person learns by practical, hands-on instruction. Conversely, an individual with a long, narrow palm and elongated, tapering, or bony fingers has a natural inclination toward theory—people with these hands couldn't be relied upon to make quick decisions, so the business world wouldn't be ideal for them. Their inclinations would be better suited in the teaching profession or in all areas of theoretical analysis. (I'll delve further into the different hand types and their innate potential in Part II.)

Applying the knowledge of a person's natural preferences and patterns to the selection of a mate could prove significant; the knowledge of palmistry can also be a significant supplement to marriage counseling by helping each partner understand the other. In this case, it will be best to focus on their similarities and on the common ground they share, rather than on their differences. (The various factors of compatibility will be outlined in Part III.)

Dermatoglyphics

Another aspect of palmistry is the study of the tiny grooves in the palm and fingertips that form distinctive patterns. The name given this specialized field is *dermatoglyphics,* which is one of the most widely accepted areas of palmistry, as it is of utmost importance in forensic criminology, where the patterns on fingertips serve as a means of identification.

The identification of the never-changing patterns engraved on fingertips is now widely used by the FBI and in forensics, but North American Indians are said to have taken finger- and handprints long before the first Europeans arrived. As an example, a huge cliff in Nova Scotia bears the carved outline of a hand, revealing skin ridges in a spiral pattern on the fingers.

In the Western world, the earliest pronouncement that finger patterns could be used for identification purposes was made in 1684, but nearly two centuries lapsed before their value in crime detection was discovered. William James Herschel, grandson of a famous British astronomer, was intrigued by the fingerprints used as signatures in ancient China. By 1860, he had become firmly convinced that no two people's fingerprints were exactly alike, not even those of identical twins. Herschel then sent his findings to Bengal's prison system, suggesting that his methods could be effectively applied for registering inmates by fingerprinting them. He was eventually recognized and even knighted for this endeavor, and has since been credited as the "founder of fingerprints."

Sir Francis Galton, who was a cousin of Charles Darwin, had gained distinction as a student of heredity—but having learned about Herschel's discovery, he immediately became absorbed in dermatoglyphics and undertook investigations on his own after long conferences with Herschel. Galton became convinced that patterns on fingertips remain unchanged throughout a person's life; in fact, he tracked the marking of one person's single fingerprint through 50 years of his life. He stated that "fingerprints are incomparably the most sure and unchanging of all forms of signatures." As a result, some authorities referred to them as *natal autographs.* These patterns are established in the fetus at four months into pregnancy and remain unchanged until the final disintegration of the epidermis after death. It's virtually impossible to obliterate these patterns, because even if burnt or injured, nature restores them to their original design.

Sir Francis Galton gave Herschel credit as originator of the fingerprinting system for identification purposes—but Galton advanced the research by separating the prints into basic patterns (which will be discussed later in this book). Galton further recorded the number of capillary ridges present in each print, which depends largely on the skin texture of the individual. In hands with a coarse skin, these patterns are clearly visible with the naked eye, while the grooves or ridges on fine skin have to be established with a microscope or a magnifying glass.

Galton's ideas for classification of basic patterns were further developed by Sir Edward Henry, who, in 1901, established the first fingerprint bureau at Scotland Yard. His work placed him among the pioneers in this field. Some years later, in 1928, another Scotland Yard expert, Harry Battley, devised a system by which separate files were made for the classification of "single" finger- or thumbprints, as well as those of the ten digits of both hands.

It was after the implementation of the fingerprint bureau at Scotland Yard that criminals tried to obliterate their prints with skin grafts and by wearing gloves during their illegal activities. Yet other countries slowly followed England's example and established similar fingerprinting offices in their prisons. As early as 1905, Sing Sing and other New York state prisons adopted fingerprinting; and the Department of Justice authorized the 60-dollar payment to inaugurate the system at the federal prison at Leavenworth, which was the first federal use of this new method. From this inconspicuous beginning, the mammoth files of the FBI grew—they're now recognized as the largest and most complete in the world.

I'd like to wrap this up with an anecdote. In America, Mark Twain's fictional story of an eccentric country lawyer, nicknamed "Pudd'nhead Wilson," first opened the eyes of many people to the importance of using fingerprints as a means of identification. *Pudd'nhead Wilson* played an immeasurable role in overcoming skepticism regarding palmistry and dermatoglyphics in this country.

The source for this book was Twain's visit to the famous Cheiro in England. Cheiro was so accurate in analyzing Twain's hands that his parting remark was: "You have just given me a great idea for my next book." The result was *Pudd'nhead Wilson*. Published in 1894, this book was written *six years before* the system for fingerprinting had been established in England.

I hope that this introduction to palmistry will inspire readers to become true believers, and that some of you will engage in studies of your own that may add building blocks of knowledge to this interesting science. There is much to learn and to discover, so let's get started!

PART I

A Manual of Modern Scientific Palmistry

CHAPTER 1

The Size and Texture of the Hand

General Information

When you become aware of the significance of hands, you'll evaluate them from an entirely different perspective than before you became interested in palmistry. Up until now, you probably scrutinized them primarily in terms of their physical attributes, lamenting the fact that your fingernails were brittle, or that you had ugly "knuckle fingers" (joints in the fingers and thumbs that are rather prominently developed). I can guarantee that after reading this book, your observation of hands will go beyond the mere aspect of physical beauty.

Which Hand Do You Analyze?

Whenever I do a reading or give a lecture, people ask the above question, and my answer is always: "Both." If a person is right-handed, then the left hand is the *birth hand,* where genetic tendencies and predispositions have left their natal imprint, while the right, or *dominant hand* registers the development from birth throughout life to a greater extent than the birth hand does.

Most palmists seem to be in agreement that if the two hands of a person are markedly different, then the dominant hand carries greater weight in the analysis. A case in point are the aforementioned hands of Oscar Wilde: Cheiro saw in his left hand a brilliant future and superior intellectual qualities, while his right hand registered Wilde's dark and negative side, which ultimately led to his downfall.

The Size of the Hands

Most people associate palmistry with the lines etched into the palmar surface, but the first consideration should be given to the shape, size, and other physical characteristics of the hand and fingers, as well as to their proportions and respective balance. This data forms the building block that allows us to determine the basic personality type and modus operandi of a person. Having established that, the lines then complement the picture, as they reveal how and where abilities and energies are being utilized.

Generally speaking, large hands and feet go together with a large body, but occasionally, small people have surprisingly large hands and vice versa. The size of the hand reveals interesting facts and provides many clues to its owner's personality. Whatever the actual size of a person's hand, its significance is overshadowed by the proportions between the hand and fingers, as well as by the width and length of the palm compared to the length of the fingers. These constitute the special features that make a hand unique.

Before we can even talk about what large versus small hands mean, we must establish what the average size of a hand is. A man's hand is considered average if it measures approximately seven inches from the tip of the middle finger—which in most hands is the longest digit—to the wrist. Anything less or more is either small or large, but once again, the build of his body must be taken into account. For a woman, the average hand measures approximately six inches from the wrist to the tip of the middle finger, or fits into a size-six glove.

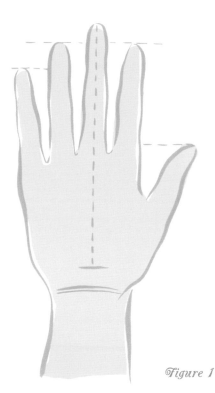

Figure 1

The Middle Finger As a Gauge

The middle finger is generally the longest digit and is used as a gauge for comparing not only the length of the fingers to the palm, but also for measuring and comparing the other fingers. An average middle finger would measure approximately ⅞ of the length of the palm, from the wrist section to the base of the middle finger (see Figure 1 on page 5). In practical terms, if the length of the palm measures 3.6 inches, the middle finger would be about 3 inches long.

Now that we've established what's average, let's find out what small or large hands reveal.

Small Hands

People whose hands are unusually small by comparison to the rest of their body "think and act big"—for instance, have you ever noticed a small person getting out of an oversized car? Individuals with small hands can sum up strangers at a glance, and they know instinctively if they can be trusted or not. Small-handed people grasp the focal points of a plan rapidly and aren't afraid to make decisions, either for themselves or for others. Such individuals prefer action and they expect results. They generally let others work out the details—especially if their fingers are also short compared to their palm. Small hands are encountered among every profession and in all walks of life, but people with small hands often gravitate toward careers where their decisive personalities and quick assessment of opportunities are valuable assets— for instance, in the business world. Individuals with small hands should avoid careers that require much routine work or close attention to details, as he or she would find such jobs too tedious and boring.

Large Hands

Large hands reveal a thoughtful and patient temperament. Such hands belong to the individual who is deliberate by nature and not in a hurry to make up his or her mind about anything. It seems a strange paradox that people with large hands should possess innate skills for doing fine, delicate work, but I once watched a pastry chef with the largest pair of hands I've ever seen fabricate the most intricate, dainty decorations.

Thick and Thin Hands

Thick and fleshy hands are easy to judge: The thicker the palm, the greater the physical stamina. These people love to be active, and it's important and beneficial for them to channel their physical and mental energies constructively.

If there's any doubt about a palm's thinness, one must observe its center. If the tendons are clearly visible, then the hand is considered thin; if it's also compressed in the middle, then palmists refer to it as "the hollow palm," suggesting a somewhat reserved and introverted personality with a limited supply of physical energy and vitality. (As always, this needs to be confirmed by other signs in the hand.)

Firm and Soft Hands

A thick hand that's firm to the touch reveals stamina and vitality, but a thick hand that feels flabby and soft indicates that the person's physical energies aren't being fully utilized. This reduces the good qualities that are ascribed to the thick hand.

If a hand is thick and hard, coupled with inflexible fingers, it goes together with an inflexible and stubborn nature. Such an individual possesses little sensitivity or genuine concern for others.

Thin hands show a measure of refinement, but if they're also very soft, they belong to people who are self-indulgent, with a tendency toward laziness. If the hands are thin, yet firm, the available energy is being used to its greatest advantage.

Skin Texture

When shaking or holding someone's hand, its texture is noticed instantly. But believe it or not, rough skin is *not* the result of hard, manual labor. We're born with a certain type of skin, which, to use an analogy, may range from very fine silk or satin to homespun linen or burlap.

Silky, smooth skin hints at a fussy, exacting nature, with a tendency to be overly critical. Such a texture belongs to the perfectionist, especially if the hand is long and bony—which also suggests a lack of empathy.

Finely textured skin is also a feature of the sensual personality; if this is the case, the hand tends to be fleshy and soft, rather than thin and bony. If the skin on the fingertips is smooth and fine, then regardless of the texture found upon the palmar surface, it suggests that its owner possesses an intuitive sixth sense.

Rough and coarse skin reflects a lack of refinement. The hands of people who work with rough materials may be callous, but that doesn't alter its *texture,* which is made up of skin or papillary ridges. Those individuals who are born with tough and leathery skin enjoy the simple, down-to-earth things in life, such as food, drink, and sensual pleasures.

The Handshake

What can you tell from a handshake? The answer is twofold, as the type of handshake relates to our physical, as well as psychological makeup, and reflects our social attitudes.

- Hands that feel **soft and "almost boneless"** display a sensual, self-gratifying nature, fond of comforts and luxuries, although their owners may not want to work for these themselves, and will expect others to provide them.

- The person with a **cool hand** is always more interested in taking rather than giving. Therefore, it reveals a certain amount of egotism and a lack of empathy for others. (Cool hands can also reveal poor circulation; in which case, one shouldn't be hasty in making such a negative assumption.)

- **Hot hands** reveal a spontaneous and rather impulsive disposition, with a tendency to be carried away by moods (unless someone has a raging fever).

- **Warm-handed** people are warm-hearted. They're similar to the hot-handed people, but are more moderate. Warm-handed people exercise greater control over their impulses and emotional reactions, but they're just as generous in spirit as people with hot hands are.

- A **firm handshake** is a sign of robust good health, vitality, and optimism. It indicates firmness of character and commitment.

- A **"crushing" handshake** suggests an overbearing personality, with a tendency to be insensitive or even cruel toward others.

The Basic Hand Types

*A*ccording to the classification of hand types developed by Casimir Stanislas d'Arpentigny in the l9th century, hands fit into six "pure" categories and one "mixed." Although this classification is still used as a guideline in modern palm reading, it's recognized that most people's hands are actually combinations of two or more types, but one category usually emerges as dominant. Generally, the shape of the palm is what determines the main hand type.

As you look at the illustrations in this chapter, the red lines shown on the palms correspond to the Life line, the green lines are the Head line, and the blue lines refer to the Heart line. I will discuss these lines and what they mean in detail in Chapter 8.

The Elementary or Clumsy Hand

This hand has a large, coarse, and thick palm, coupled with short, stubby fingers and short nails (see Figure 2). The skin texture of the palm and fingers is also coarse, showing clearly visible skin ridges. Nature has provided these for tactility, since a person with such a hand would be best suited for manual labor or for handling rough surfaces. The palmar surface shows only the major line of Life, and short or nonexistent Head and Heart lines. The thumb is extremely short, barely reaching the first section of the index finger when the hand is closed. A short thumb is a regressive sign, seen on the hands of primates. If the top, or nail, section of the thumb is heavy or bulbous, this points to a violent temper, which a person with this type of mentality would be unable to

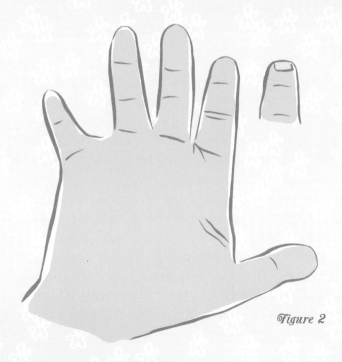

Figure 2

control. Should he commit an act of aggression or murder, it would be in a passionate fury rather than a premeditated deed.

The owner of such a hand would most likely have a perfect indifference about everything except his basic needs for survival. He'd possess little imagination or ambition, yet would likely be shrewd and cunning in providing for his livelihood. Since this hand belongs to the "Earth" type (see Chapter 20), such a person would be best suited for farming, hunting, or unskilled manual labor.

To compensate for some of their negative features, people with this hand type are fiercely loyal to their families and communities. They also have an inborn need to protect those weaker than themselves, such as children and animals. Such people are guided primarily by instinct rather than reason, behaving much as the higher animals do.

The Square or Useful Hand

In its purest form, the Square hand has a broad, square palm with fingers that are set squarely on it. The placement of the fingers is seen in Figure 3; fingers in this hand type tend to be thick and square with broad fingertips, with fingernails that are more wide than they are long. People with this type of hand tend to respect law and order, and are practical and precise in manner, less from inborn grace than from the need for conformity and habits. Through perseverance and the strength of a plodding will, they often bypass other more brilliant people in success and achievement. They remain loyal and

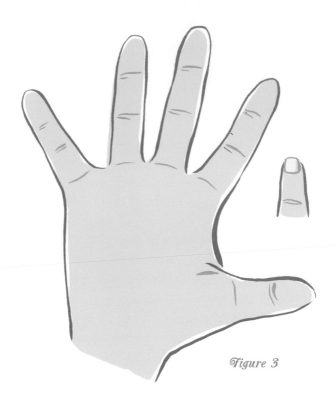

Figure 3

honest, even in the face of adversity. Their strongest short-coming is that they perceive things as either "black or white"—"shades of gray" elude them, and they only understand that which can be explained by reason and logic. Consequently, they appear to be obstinate and intolerant and might even be called "pigheaded" at times.

The Square Palm with Long Fingers

This hand shows a greater propensity toward theory, yet its bearer makes decisions based on reason and logical deductions. It isn't surprising to find many engineers, builders, and architects with this type of hand.

The Square Palm with Long, Knotty Fingers

Fingers with well-developed joints show a love of detail and an inclination toward analytical reasoning. If such a hand is encountered among people in the medical profession, it likely belongs to a specialist or a researcher, since these individuals strive for perfection.

The Square Palm with Spatulate Fingers

Fingers that are flared and wider at the tip are referred to as *spatulate* and are often seen in hands where the palm is of a slightly triangular shape. Such spatulate fingertips belong to inventors; they tend to either improve on standard practices or invent something new. However, their inventions are always on a practical plane, as indicated by the square shape of the palm.

The Square Palm with Rounded Fingertips

Fingers that have rounded, or conic, tips combine practical goals with an artistic bent, be it in music, literature, or the arts. Rounded fingertips are also indicative of well-developed social skills. This is a favorable combination to have, for such individuals will be able to use their skills to the greatest advantage.

The Square Palm with Psychic Fingers

Psychic fingers are long and taper toward the tip. This combination of palm and fingers is rarely seen, since it would bring opposites together, resulting in a complex personality. Long, pointed fingers and almond-shaped nails generally belong to the contemplative and passive, rather than to the action-loving person. Hypothetically, someone with a square palm and psychic fingers would give in to capriciousness. An example of this is an artist who has a studio full of unfinished paintings.

The Square Palm with Mixed Fingers

As a rule, all fingers don't have identical tips. The index and little fingers (and often the ring finger as well) are more tapered than the middle finger. However, if the shapes of fingers and thumbs vary excessively, the hand is referred to as "mixed." If accompanied by a supple thumb with a strong outward bent, it reflects an extremely versatile personality, but the squareness of the palm would allow its owner to see the practical side of things as well. Yet, since people with this hand type tend to lack persistence, they'll rarely rise to great heights of success.

The Spatulate or Energetic Hand

The Spatulate hand is given this name because the shape of the palm resembles a spatula and the fingers are wider at the tips (see Figure 4). If the palm is wider at the wrist section, the person is full of restless physical energy;

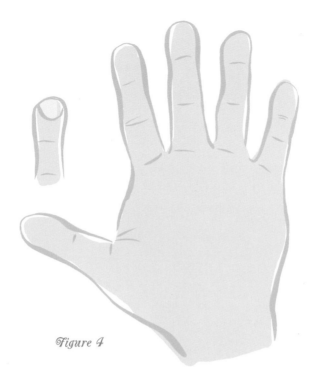

Figure 4

if the palm is wider at the base of the fingers, he makes full use of his keen ability for logical deductions. In either case, people with spatulate palms and/or fingers have a fidgety quality, coupled with a love of action. Wherever this hand is encountered, its owner is endowed with individuality and ingenuity.

As a rule, the Spatulate hand is medium to large, with well-developed fingers. The nails may be of varied shapes; if they're on the short side, such a person has a tendency to be impatient and critical.

One of the most striking characteristics of people with the Spatulate hand is the need for independence and individuality. As a result, they generally choose to own their own business, for which their pioneering spirit is well suited.

In relationships, owners of the Spatulate hand are known for loyalty and honesty, but they need enough room to breathe, otherwise they will resent the ties.

The Philosophic or Intellectual Hand

The shape of this hand is easily recognized. It's characterized by a lengthy, angular palm with long, bony fingers that have well-developed joints that are generally

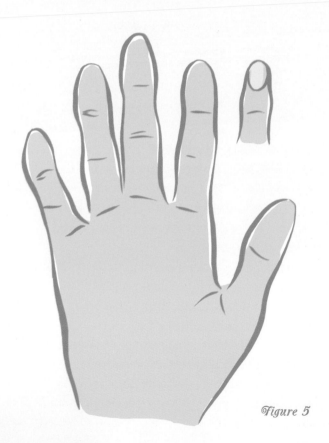

Figure 5

accompanied by long fingernails (see Figure 5). The palmar surface is usually marked with many additional lines besides the major ones of Life, Head, and Heart.

These hands belong to scholars, deep thinkers, and poets. They belong to lovers of detail, who weigh each decision very carefully and extensively, so much so that in waiting for just the right moment to act, they might miss opportunities altogether. People with these hands have a natural leaning toward law and order, especially if the finger joints are well developed and if the middle finger is of at least average length.

Hands of the Philosophic/Intellectual type can be found everywhere and among all professions. In the field of medicine, such a person would be ideally suited for research, especially if the finger joints are defined, which reflects patience for detail and a tendency toward perfectionism. It's unlikely that people with these hands would be drawn toward practicing "general medicine," since they might lack the jovial manners and gregariousness of a "country doctor." This isn't to say that the owner of this hand type lacks feelings, but their concern would most likely be for humankind rather than for the individual patient.

The Long, Angular Palm with Smooth Fingers

Long, smooth, and tapering fingers would indicate the opposite of the above, as such fingers express quick, intuitive perceptions and responses—it's no wonder that yogis and spiritual leaders quite often display such long, tapering fingers.

If the palm is extremely elongated, it reveals a very sensitive nature, one that may be somewhat removed from reality. This tendency is further enhanced if the palmar surface is crisscrossed by a host of fine lines, for the balance of the person's energies is unevenly distributed.

The Conic/Artistic Hand

As a rule, this hand is medium-sized, with a rounded palm that tapers slightly toward the base of the fingers, forming a gentle arch. The palm and fingers are generally of a smooth texture and end in rounded fingertips and nails (see Figure 6). If the fingers are full at the base section, it reveals a love of luxury and comfort.

The main characteristics of the Conic hand are spontaneity and intuition. People possessing this type of hand

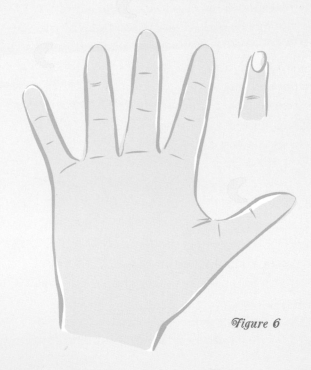

Figure 6

are quick in thought and ideas and also tend to be witty conversationalists. They grasp the meaning of a subject rapidly, but are often satisfied with a superficial knowledge of it. Generally, people with this hand type don't become scholars, for they like to spread themselves thinly over a large area, rather than concentrate on one subject. Individuals with this hand type also have a tendency to form judgments quickly based on their hunches and first impressions of people and situations—which isn't to say that they aren't right at times, but hunches certainly aren't infallible.

Individuals with the Conic/Artistic hand are generous by nature; they give freely, often on the spur of the moment. This hand is also referred to as *Social/Artistic,* more for the sociability of its owner than for the expression of artistic ideas.

If the Conic hand is firm and elastic, it brings out the best qualities of its type. This indicates greater energy and strength of will than the hand that is soft and pudgy and has an exaggerated development of the Mounts (which will be fully discussed in Chapter 7). Conic hands are often encountered among actors, politicians, and public speakers; they also belong to those people who are engaged in "emotional careers," including sales-oriented professions, as these people possess an inborn feel for public awareness. They tend to respond to inspirations of the moment before they consciously use reason and logic.

The Conic Hand with Square Fingers

People with this combination may rise to fame and fortune faster than those with the pure Conic hand. Success will be achieved by different means, such as by the application of energy and endurance. Individuals with this hand are exact in their methods and work habits, and their inherent staying power will help them fulfill their expectations.

The Conic Hand with Spatulate Fingers

This combination of palm and fingers adds an innovative and individualistic touch to everything its owner undertakes. It's said that actors should have a spatulate third, or "ring," finger in order to go beyond mediocrity in their profession!

The Psychic/Intuitive Hand

This is the most beautiful and elegant of all of the hand types, but it's also the most impractical to possess, according to many palmists. The Psychic/Intuitive hand is characterized by a lengthy, narrow palm, coupled with long, tapering fingers with almond-shaped nails. (See Figure 7.) When shaking hands with such a person, the hand feels almost boneless, and one is afraid of crushing it with a firm handshake. The delicate structure and beauty of such a hand suggests a lack of robust strength—one fears that its owner would be ill equipped for a harsh life.

Individuals with the pure form of the Psychic hand possess a visionary, idealistic nature. They appreciate beauty in all areas, and their aesthetic sense will take preference above all else, especially practicality. Generally, people with such hands are trustworthy and gentle in manner; so much so that they may become easy prey for ruthless people. Since their sensitive and intuitive faculties are so highly developed, such hands may be encountered among mediums and clairvoyants.

People who have children born with the Psychic hand type don't understand them unless they themselves possess a similar personality; if they don't, those children grow up feeling misunderstood and melancholy. Practically oriented parents may try to guide their children into careers that they're unsuited for, such as business-oriented or technical professions. More appropriate career choices would lie in the fields of decorating, music, acting, and the arts.

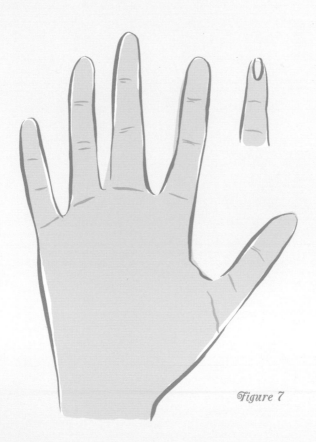

Figure 7

The Mixed Hand

This hand is the most difficult to describe and to recognize, since it varies from person to person. The Mixed hand doesn't seem to belong to any of the previously mentioned types, since its fingers are too varied to fit into one or two categories (see Figure 8).

The Mixed hand is indicative of a versatile person with a wealth of ideas. Taken to extremes, it's reflective of a changeable and volatile personality. Individuals with such hands may be adaptable with regard to people and circumstances; in fact, they may be so adaptable that they

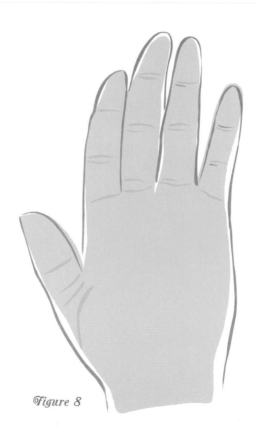

Figure 8

don't seem to have a mind of their own. Such people may be brilliant conversationalists, with the ability to discuss any topic superficially—but they may lack in-depth knowledge about any one subject in particular. Owners of such hands may also be inventive or artistic, and are likely to be known as "Jacks-of-all trades."

The linear pattern on the palm will help to determine whether this versatility can be interpreted positively as brilliant or creative, or unfavorably as a lack of conviction and self-control. (I'll discuss the lines on the palm further in Part II.)

People possessing a Mixed hand may find their niche in the diplomatic corps, as negotiators, in public relations, or in the performing arts, where their versatility and inborn adaptability will be an asset.

Now that we've seen the classification of the basic hand types, examining the individual fingers will add another dimension to the diversity that exists in the human hand.

The Individual Fingers

he names given to the fingers are significant in their interpretation and are in keeping with palmistry's link to astrology. Each finger rules over a particular sphere and must be considered first separately, then in correlation to the other fingers, and finally, as relating to the rest of the hand.

- The index finger is called **"Jupiter,"** or the "world finger." It measures leadership potential and our attitudes toward the "world at large."

- The middle finger is named **"Saturn,"** and is used as a gauge by which not only the other fingers are judged, but the length of the palm as well (see Figure I, page 5). Saturn also reflects our attitudes toward law and order, home, traditions, and stability.

CHAPTER 3

- The ring finger is called **"Apollo,"** and is connected to the arts; it also measures innate creative abilities. This finger was chosen to wear wedding or engagement rings, symbolizing our intimate commitments with other people.

- The little finger is named **"Mercury,"** and is often referred to as the "messenger." This is the sphere that's associated with all types of expression and communication, dating from our earliest relationships, where we bonded with our parents and family.

The Finger Sections

Fingers are divided into three sections, called "phalanges." When the fingers are of average length, each phalange is approximately equal in size—but you'll be surprised to see how differently proportioned these phalanges can be. The phalanges give special meaning to our preferences and tendencies.

- The top section is also referred to as the **"nail phalange."** It relates to the realm of mental and spiritual perceptions.

- The second or **"middle phalange"** deals with our ability to find practical, viable solutions and applications for our ideas.

- The third or **"base phalange"** reveals physical, sexual, and instinctual needs, values, and traditions.

The Jupiter Finger

This finger shows how we see ourselves in relation to the outside world. It stands for "me, myself, and I." Jupiter is the finger of assertion and is often used by people who are stressing their point of view—however, a short Jupiter finger is unlikely to be used in this fashion. A parent may admonish a child by wagging their index finger back and forth, showing displeasure at something the child has done.

- If Jupiter is short by comparison to the second and third fingers—that is, if it doesn't reach the middle of the nail phalange of Saturn, this person isn't likely to seek leadership or responsibility for others. If it's excessively long, the opposite is true.

- A long Jupiter finger on a broad, Useful hand shows that the person has no fear of the future or of making decisions. They're neither afraid of authority nor of exercising it.

- If a long Jupiter is encountered on a narrow, Intuitive hand type, it signifies a desire to dominate loved ones, usually due to fear and lack of confidence.

- If Jupiter leans toward Saturn, this reveals an attitude of caution and an inward-directed flow of energy—if extreme, it could even be an indication of agoraphobia or "street fear." This person may also love acquisitions, which constitutes a conscious or subconscious compensation for an inferiority complex.

- Where the top or nail phalange is short compared to the same sections of the other fingers, criticism from others is resented, pointing to an overly sensitive nature.

- Salesmen, teachers, and lecturers should have long and tapering first phalanges, for this signifies a probing and inquiring type of mind, as well as a facility for verbal expression and an innate gift for influencing others.

- If the nail phalange is square-tipped, its owner thrives on law and order, which would explain why such fingertips are often seen in the hands of lawyers, judges, and policemen.

- If the second or middle phalange is long, the person is a great planner and organizer, making full use of ideas—this would be an asset for many professions, especially for an executive.

- Where the third or base phalange is large and firm, it reveals a desire toward physical domination over others, using "brawn over brain." This could be seen in the hands of animal trainers, foremen, or despots.

- A flabby third phalange is a sign of excessive self-indulgence—*quantity* rather than *quality* is preferred here.

- If one phalange is noticeably shorter than average, the positive values represented by that section are reduced. For instance, a short middle phalange on the Jupiter finger would show a lack of practical abilities.

- Rings worn on the right Jupiter finger are a clear announcement that the person likes to be in charge. If worn on the left finger, it indicates that they desire to be in command in their private life or domain. For example, pictures of Henry VIII show that he wore rings on both of his index fingers.

- A crooked or twisted finger—unless caused by an injury or arthritic conditions—isn't a favorable sign. A long, crooked finger reveals that its owner would use any method, even an unscrupulous one, in order to achieve their aim.

The Saturn Finger

Physically speaking, this finger is the most firmly rooted of all. It represents the serious part in people and is associated with law, order, and stability. The Saturn finger should measure approximately ⅞ of the length of the palm, and it should be approximately half a phalange longer than Jupiter and Apollo to be considered average (see Figure 1, page 5). This constitutes a good balance between seriousness and lightheartedness.

- If the Saturn finger towers over the other fingers, this would belong to someone with a morbid imagination, who is unable to see the bright side of things. Such a personality would be referred to as "Saturnine."

- If the fingers on either side seem to withdraw from Saturn, this reveals antisocial tendencies. Such a person would show little regard for home and stability. When the tip of Saturn bends toward the Apollo finger, a degree of introspection is expressed.

- A long nail phalange of Saturn, especially if flexible at the first joint, signifies an interest in psychic phenomena or awareness. This may be encountered in the hands of psychics, mediums, or clairvoyants, as well as in people possessing a sixth sense.

- If the second phalange dominates this finger, a strong tendency toward science and mathematics is indicated, yet this isn't restricted to those professions. A long second section of Saturn may be encountered in the hands of nature lovers as well.

- If the third phalange is the dominant section, this points to someone with traditional values. If this section is long and thin, it may reveal a preference for expensive home furnishings; if long and broad, quantity takes preference over quality.

- If the third phalange is short and fat, the discriminating factor is absent, and greed would likely take its place. When gaps appear at the bases of such fat third-finger sections, the person has difficulty holding on to cash. As a rule, spaces between fingers are only evident if the base sections are thin.

- Knotty finger joints are an indication of a philosophical nature, as they stem the flow of the person's impulses.

- A square fingertip of Saturn, regardless of the other fingertips, signifies an interest in legal matters and a respect for law and order in general.

- Rounded fingertips on Saturn indicate an affinity for numbers, which is an excellent asset for the hands of an accountant.

- If rings are worn on this finger—regardless of whether it's the left or right hand—this reveals a need for security.

The Apollo Finger

This is also referred to as the "Sun" or "Success" finger, as it expresses our inborn creativity; it's also the sphere that measures personal relationships. The left or "private" Apollo finger was selected centuries ago to wear marriage and engagement rings, symbolizing our emotional commitments.

The size, shape, and position of Apollo holds important information with regard to our basic attitudes. A distinctive Apollo of at least average length, at approximately the same level as Jupiter, reveals a person's appreciation of beauty and harmony in all forms, from creation in nature to "man-made" works of art.

- If Apollo pulls away from the Saturn finger, the individual tends to gravitate toward an unorthodox or unconventional lifestyle.

- If Apollo leans toward Saturn, it reflects a need for security; and if it should even cling to Saturn, it reveals an excessive dependency on emotional or financial security.

- When the Apollo finger is shorter than average, its owners find it difficult to make decisions that involve taking any chances, and they don't tend to like gambling in any shape or form. People with shorter-than-average Apollo fingers may still be successful, but they need to work for it, as success isn't likely to fall in their laps.

- The opposite holds true if the Apollo finger is much longer than average, occasionally even surpassing the Saturn finger in length. People possessing such fingers are risk takers, especially if the Apollo finger appears on a hand with an overly flexible, arched thumb (discussed in the next chapter).

- If the fingertip section of Apollo is long, then the artistic sense is highly developed, especially if the tip is tapered or rounded.

- If the first phalange is long and spatulate, this indicates an inborn gift for storytelling and performing. In fact, it's believed that to be a gifted actor, the Apollo finger should have a spatulate formation. Such flared fingertips may be encountered among all professions, from tailors to carpenters to architects, and chances are, these people bring a special inventiveness and ingenuity to their work.

- If the first phalange is long and broad, it signifies an ability to make money in a big way; here, practical consideration is overriding the aesthetic sense.

- An actor or someone who can perform mimicry or impersonations is likely to have a slender and long second phalange. Such people are also seen to be "quick-witted." A long second phalange further suggests a good color sense.

- A long, slender third or base phalange reveals inborn good taste that may be expressed in the individual's home furnishings and clothing. A short, fat phalange would signify the opposite, however.

- A long, broad third phalange that's firm and not flabby reveals a healthy enjoyment of the good things in life, but not to excess. Such a phalange would be encountered in the hands of food or wine connoisseurs.

- A well-developed Apollo of at least average length, coupled with a hand that's broad at the wrist, belongs to a physically and mentally well-balanced individual. This formation may be seen in the hands of athletes who have a positive attitude toward winning and are confident in competition.

The Mercury Finger

This is the sphere of expression and communication. As seen in Figure 9, the average-sized Mercury finger reaches to the base of the nail phalange of Apollo, unless the Mercury finger is set unusually low in the palm, which will be discussed later in this chapter in "Finger Setting."

The Mercury finger reveals our attitudes toward relationships, but especially toward our very first bonding with our parents. Any aberration here, such as a twisted or crooked Mercury, could provide a clue to early problems. Such a formation points to lack of honesty or a "twisted mentality." Sadly, these negative characteristics are often rooted in childhood traumas.

- People who possess a well-developed top phalange have an inborn knack for communication—such people are natural teachers, sales professionals, actors, public speakers, and politicians.

- If the nail phalange is the longest of the three sections, then the person is persuasive—even more so if Mercury leans toward the Apollo finger. In this case, the person wouldn't be averse to stretching a point in order to reach their goals. As Mercury is also referred to as the "finger of enterprise," a long, tapering finger enhances intuitive perceptions in all areas of communication.

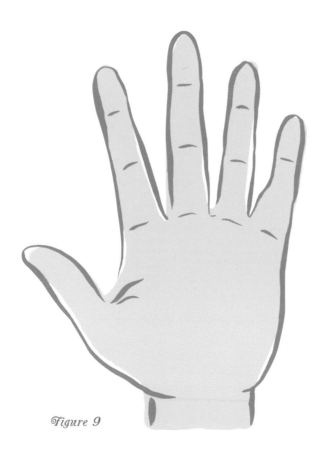

Figure 9

- Rounded tips on the Mercury finger are an indication of good language and social skills. These would be an asset in the hands of those in the nursing, teaching, or public relations fields.

- Knotty finger joints on Mercury, as in all fingers, show a love of law and order. Since such joints slow down the flow of impulses and spontaneity, they tend to belong to people with a deliberate and analytical mind-set.

- If the entire Mercury finger is wide and sturdy, its owner is generally broad-minded and possesses a "live-and-let-live" attitude toward others.

- A long, bony, and thin Mercury finger, coupled with a broad palm, reveals that its owner isn't easily aroused sexually, while such a finger on a thin, dry palm indicates a lack of sexual interest altogether. Rings on this finger, especially if worn by men, suggest some peculiarity regarding intimate relationships—which is generally rooted in a lack of parental bonding.

- If the top and second sections are pressed in toward the Apollo finger, this is an indication of a self-indulgent nature, especially if the third or base phalange is also fat and puffy.

- If the third section is enlarged on the inside of the finger toward the Apollo finger (as seen in Figure 9), it indicates a conflict of loyalties between the person's first family—that is, parents and siblings—and subsequent relationships, such as with a spouse and even children. If one of the marriage partners displays such a "stepped-in" formation, there will always be conflicts. When encountered in the hands of young people, it may prevent them from leaving "the nest."

The Fingertips

There are four basic shapes of fingertips:

1. Tapered/Pointed
2. Conic/Rounded
3. Square
4. Spatulate

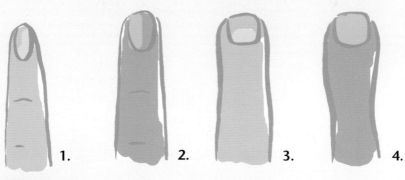

Figure 10

It's unlikely that one hand will display identical fingertips on all the fingers, but it would be unusual to find extreme shapes together, such as very tapered with square or spatulate fingertips. Such opposites would be found in the "Mixed" hand type.

1. Tapered/Pointed

With such fingertips, impressions and vibrations from the outside enter uninterrupted—the result is that such people perceive ideas rapidly and instinctively and reply with like responses. As a rule, these individuals pay meticulous attention to details; in fact, patience with minutiae, and with people, seems to be their trademark.

2. Conic/Rounded

People who possess these fingertips have a personality that works smoothly and without friction. They need beauty and harmony in their surroundings in order to be happy. Rounded fingertips belong to socially adept individuals who have an inborn sense of balance; their peace-loving nature extends to all of their relationships.

3. Square

With square fingertips, vibrations and impressions received from the outside world slow down. Therefore, square-tipped fingers belong to people who are deliberate and practical—they focus on their work with a single-mindedness, whether they're cabinet makers or dentists.

4. Spatulate

The flow of energy emanating from the outside has to break down the greatest resistance when entering this type of fingertip—creating friction, agitation, and excitement. People with spatulate fingertips should have some form of physical outlet, since they have an abundance of pent-up physical and mental energy that needs constant challenge. Such people are endowed with individuality and originality, but they're not known for exercising patience. They also don't tend to accept conventional answers, which makes them appear stubborn and obstinate at times.

If individuals with spatulate palms and/or fingertips choose the teaching profession, they could be fascinating educators, since they would most likely be able to stimulate and hatch innovative ideas among students.

The Finger Setting

It's important to observe how the fingers are arranged on the palm. A good way to determine the setting is to draw a line across the palm from the Jupiter to the Mercury finger.

The four basic settings are described below.

1. The Uneven Setting

This is the most common finger setting to have. Here, the Jupiter and Saturn fingers are almost at the same base level, the Apollo finger drops down slightly, and Mercury

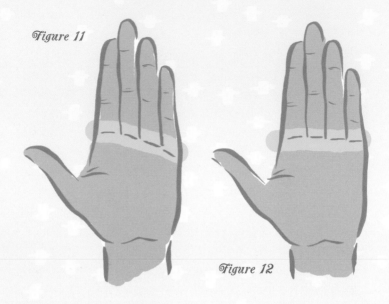

Figure 11

Figure 12

is somewhat lower than the others (see Figure 11). A low-set Mercury reduces the favorable qualities ascribed to this finger—if set very low on the palm, this implies that its owner is selecting a difficult approach to life, since a low Mercury restricts the ability to communicate, especially in relation to intimate relationships. In many hands, this finger would be quite tall, but by virtue of its low setting, it appears rather short.

One of the interpretations of the uneven setting is that the person has been unable to reach their full potential in one area or another. It seems a strange paradox that a number of writers and poets have deep-set Mercury fingers; most likely, they turned to writing because they were unable to express themselves adequately through the spoken word.

It's important to examine both hands of a person. A low-set Mercury on the left hand only would indicate that the person is unable to express themselves fully emotionally; while on their right hand, the Mercury finger may be set higher, showing that they have no problem with communication in the professional or nonpersonal areas. Very low-set Mercury fingers in both hands would signify that this person's lack of self-confidence would permeate their entire life.

2. The Square Setting

If the fingers are set squarely on the palm, this person shows no lack of confidence, and may, in fact, be arrogant (see Figure 12). Since those with square finger settings believe themselves to be invincible and infallible, they usually manage to achieve their goals. In the hands of sales people, this setting promises a strong success rate, especially if it's coupled with strongly developed Mercury and Jupiter fingers. The negative side of this setting is that such people can be overbearing and insufferable.

3. The Rounded Setting

When the fingers are set in a gentle arch, it reflects a good mental balance (see Figure 13). These people aren't arrogant, nor do they suffer from a lack of confidence. This type of finger setting is often encountered in the Conic hand, since people with this hand type are socially adept and avoid confrontations whenever possible. However, they will stand up for their beliefs if they need to.

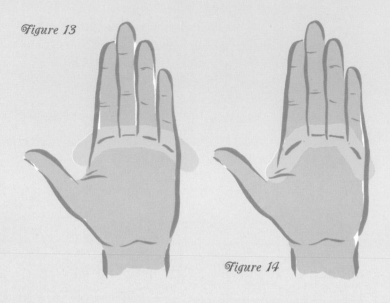

Figure 13

Figure 14

4. Low-Set Jupiter and Mercury Fingers

If both Jupiter and Mercury fingers are set low, this suggests problem areas, especially as Jupiter represents the ego, and a low setting would point to a lack of self-esteem (see Figure 14). A low-set Jupiter in the left or "birth" hand only would signify that a person's feelings of inadequacy are confined to their personal life. If such a setting is in the right hand only, it would involve their professional career, but if present in both hands, the lack of confidence would permeate the entire personality.

Flexibility vs. Inflexibility

Flexible fingers are synonymous with a flexible mind. People who possess them are unconventional and inquisitive. Security and position aren't the most important things in their life, but on the negative side, these people may let cash and opportunities slip easily through their flexible fingers.

Fingers that bend at the top joint express a tolerant attitude toward others. Such people are born with insight and understanding, while a pliable second phalange indicates flexibility in more mundane, practical matters.

If the fingers can be bent back and forth like rubber, such individuals are very impressionable, with a tendency to be open-minded, as well as "open-mouthed," for they like to gossip.

The opposite holds true for extremely stiff and unbending fingers, which tend to accompany a rigid nature; such people have little use for social amenities and tact. This is especially noteworthy when examining the thumb, which is the most important finger in our hand. In fact, some ancient Chinese scholars of palmistry concentrated their entire studies on this digit.

Let's take a closer look at why the thumb is so important.

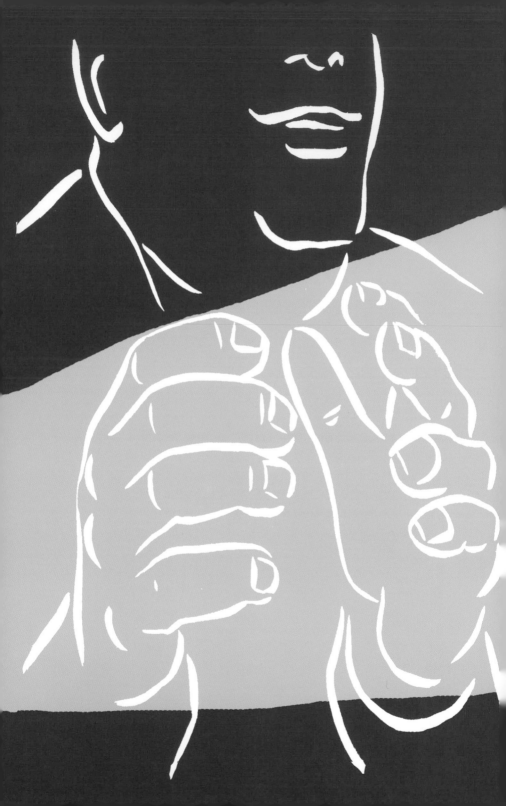

The Importance of the Thumb

*T*he thumb is itself a finger, but it's infinitely more than that. If one of our thumbs became injured, we'd quickly realize just how vital it was for our daily functioning. According to anthropologists, the thumb "individualizes" human beings—the theory is that as apes evolved into humans, they employed the thumb first for holding and throwing stones; later, it became useful for manufacturing tools, utensils, and fine instruments. An imprint of an orangutan's hand (see Figure 15, page 48) illustrates that while its palm and fingers are remarkably similar to ours, its hand is characterized by a very short and low-set thumb. Therefore, the logical deduction would be that the longer and stronger the thumb, the more highly evolved the personality.

CHAPTER 4

In the East, where the science of palmistry was first established and held in high esteem, some scholars devoted their entire lives to studying the thumb, asserting that it held all of the answers to an individual's personality and health, and that its possibilities were unlimited.

Figure 15

Midwives also recognized the importance of the thumb; in fact, it was one of the areas they would closely monitor on newborns. If an infant's hand remained closed up over their thumb for too long, the midwife would get concerned about the baby's mental and physical well-being. Even today, a person who clenches their hand over their thumb, or hides it inside their fist like a newborn does, is seen to reveal extreme discomfort, anguish, or fear.

The Sections of the Thumb

The thumb has two sections or phalanges (see Figure 16).

- As we saw in the last chapter with the other fingers, the thumb's first or "nail" phalange is associated with its owner's mental qualities, which includes their will.

- The second phalange correlates with logic, powers of rationalization, relating, and implementing ideas.

- The third section of the thumb (which is not a phalange) relates to the physical aspects of sensuality and vitality.

The Length of the Thumb

A thumb of average length (see Figure 1, page 5) reaches to the middle of the base section of the Jupiter finger when measured against it. The length of the thumb can be deceiving, depending on whether it's set low or high in the hand—for instance, a person with a low-set thumb (starting almost from the wrist) tends to live more by instinct than by logic—but it's the overall length and strength of the thumb that indicates how capable, determined, and persistent its owner is.

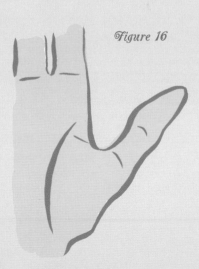

Figure 16

- The thumb resembles the root and trunk of a tree—if it's sturdy and powerful, for instance, then these qualities tend to show up in the person, too. So, people with strong thumbs will most likely triumph, even in the face of tremendous adversity.

- People with short, clumsy, low-set, or bulbous thumbs tend to be coarse, brutish, and animal-like in their behavior. This type of thumb belongs primarily to the Elementary hand type, although its variations may be found among other hand types as well.

- The opposite holds true for long, well-shaped, and balanced thumbs: Such people are endowed with inborn refinement, and they use their intellect, rather than brute force, to achieve their goals.

- If the thumb sections are unevenly developed—if, for example, a first phalange is much longer than the second—then the person's will tends to take preference over logical deduction. Consequently, they would have a tendency to be impulsive and make rash decisions.

- If the second thumb section is much longer than the first, then these individuals will tend to lack decisive qualities. Hamlet wrestled with such indecisiveness ("To be or not to be"), and so, this type of thumb is referred to as the "Hamlet Thumb."

- If the second phalange is thin and stream-lined, it's sometimes called the "wasted thumb." Despite its name, such a thumb is indicative of tact and refinement.

The Shape of the Thumb

In order to best determine the shape of the thumb you're examining, draw an outline of it on a sheet of paper. You may notice that there are many variations in thumb shapes, but listed below are the four most common types.

1. The Thick-Set, Sturdy Thumb

This type of thumb generally belongs to people whose approach to problems and dealings with others is direct and forthright (see Figure 17). This characteristic can border on stubbornness and tactlessness, depending on the degree of stiffness and thickness of the thumb. This type of thumb is most often encountered among the Square or Spatulate hand types.

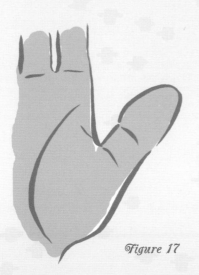

Figure 17

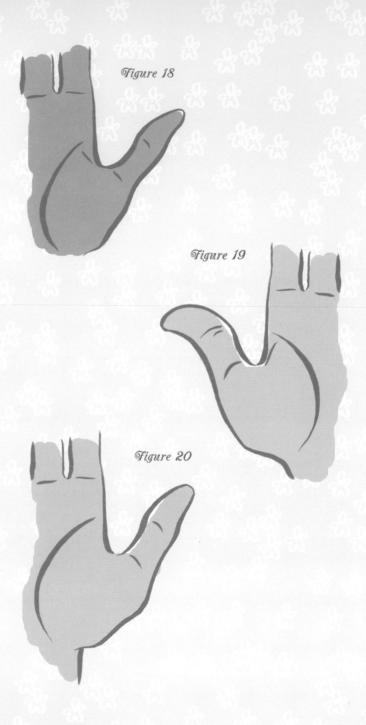

Figure 18

Figure 19

Figure 20

2. The Slender Thumb

A slender and high-set thumb is often seen among the Intellectual/Philosophic, Conic/Artistic, or Psychic/Intuitive hand types (see Figure 18). This shape implies a certain refinement, coupled with inborn tact and diplomacy, especially if the second section is graceful and streamlined.

3. The Arched Thumb

This type of thumb is the opposite of the thick-set and sturdy type (see Figure 19). The very pliable thumb is suggestive of versatility and flexibility; when arched away from the hand at an extreme angle, it reveals a tendency toward gambling and taking risks. Such people may also have difficulty holding on to cash.

4. The Musical Thumb

According to David Brandon-Jones's book *Practical Palmistry,* people with this kind of thumb, which has the base joint protruding at an acute angle, possess an inborn sense of timing and rhythm (see Figure 20). Speaking from my own experience, I once attended a large family gathering and did indeed observe that the branch of the family known for musical talent and excellent dancing all possessed this type of thumb.

The Thumb Tips

The nail section symbolizes the will of the individual. Without the benefit of a strong first phalange of at least average length, a person's abilities may not be fully realized. As an example, an average-sized thumb with a short first section and an excessively long second phalange would most likely belong to a person who has difficulty making decisions—consequently, such a person may be missing out on some wonderful opportunities.

The opposite holds true with a disproportionally long nail section, which suggests that owners make their decisions primarily based on their wants and desires, not by logic.

There are too many different thumb tips and variations to describe them all here. Below are the most basic types with regard to shapes and fullness.

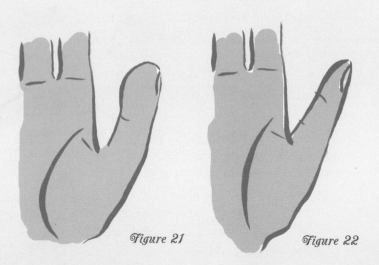

Figure 21   *Figure 22*

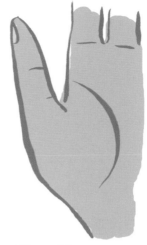

Figure 23   Figure 24

- A well-padded thumb tip reflects a reservoir of physical and mental energy (see Figure 21). Such people are generally in control of themselves and don't lose their composure easily, but when they do, watch out!

- The flattened thumb tip belongs to someone who thrives on nervous energy but loses steam quickly—when their energy is depleted, they need to lie low until their stamina is replenished (see Figure 22).

- The long, broad thumb tip belongs to people who wield executive power, those who have the necessary ability and desire to be responsible for others (see Figure 23). If these qualities are in abundance, then such individuals need to be in absolute command at all times and in all situations.

- A long, thin thumb tip is the opposite of the above—such people would be content to direct the action from the sidelines rather than take charge or seek the spotlight (see Figure 24, page 55).

- While a broad top joint of the thumb indicates a keen mentality, the thumb that ends in a pointed tip belongs to people who concentrate with razor-sharp persistence on a target (see Figure 25). They won't quit until they've accomplished their goals or intentions.

- A coarse, heavy-looking thumb tip tends to belong to people lacking tact, diplomacy, and self-control (see Figure 26). The extreme shape of this thumb is referred to as the "murderer's thumb" by many palmists. One would expect this type to belong to the most primitive and Elementary hand, and it generally does, but it may also be encountered

Figure 25   *Figure 26*

among other categories. Wherever it makes its appearance, it signifies a hot and often uncontrolled temper.

- The conic/rounded thumb tip shows good taste and a discriminating personality (see Figure 6, page 20). Unlike the "arrowhead-tip" described in Figure 25, rounded finger-tips belong to people who are adventurous and love variety.

- Square tips (see Figure 3, page 14) are generally encountered with a square palm. People with these fingertips use the "common sense" approach to life, but unlike the "stubborn" thumbs described in Figures 21 and 26 (pages 54 and 56), these people are willing to listen to someone else's point of view.

- The spatulate tip (see Figure 4, page 17) is most often encountered in the Spatulate hand type. As described in previous chapters, this shape is reflective of the most innovative and independent personality types.

Flexibility and Resistance

These characteristics are almost as much national traits as they are individual ones. For example, more supple thumbs are found among the Asian cultures and Latin nations than in Northern Europe. Such national prototypes of thumbs reflect the climatic influence on the physical and emotional development of its inhabitants over thousands of years.

In the United States, which is a melting pot of all nations, there's evidence of a wide variety of thumb tips, from the very supple to the stiff-jointed types.

The Supple Thumb

The supple thumb—including the double-jointed thumb that can be rotated backward at an extreme angle—tends to belong to extravagant people, not only in terms of money, but also with regard to their lifestyles. People with this thumb type will adjust relatively quickly and effortlessly in new situations.

The Firm-Jointed Thumb

Almost the opposite holds true for people with a firm- or stiff-jointed thumb. These people are practical rather than frivolous, and tend to be much more cautious about anything new or untried. Although they're less versatile by nature than supple-jointed individuals, these people make up for this shortcoming by being dependable and loyal in friendships . . . although they're not demonstrative when it comes to showing affection.

The stiff-jointed thumb is the extreme type of this category and therefore not nearly as favorable, since it belongs to people who are unyielding and inflexible in their outlook on life.

Depending on the rest of the hand, a firm thumb is often needed to lend stability or control to a hand that otherwise lacks firmness, as in one that's either too soft or too pliable.

Check for Resistance

A good test for the analyst is to apply pressure against the thumb of the person being evaluated by pushing against it with their own thumb. If the client's thumb offers resistance, it reveals a measure of self-control, which is a favorable sign.

If the thumb is of the very flexible type seen in Figure 19 (the Arched thumb, page 52), firmness at its base joint is an excellent feature to have, since it provides the control needed to hold extravagance in check.

The Fingernails

$\mathcal{N}$ot only do people's fingernails provide valuable information regarding their vitality and temperament—they also provide a glimpse into the present state of their health. This is true for all types and sizes of nails.

The Shape and Length of Nails

To be considered "average," fingernails' length, from the cuticle to the fingertip, should measure approximately half of the nail section. But once you become familiar with nails, you'll be amazed to see the variations that exist!

- Shorter-than-average nails are indicative of a personality that's full of "vim and vigor" (see Figure 27). People who possess this type of nails are quick-witted . . . and quite often have a temper to match. They also tend to be very critical—of others *and* of themselves. There's no doubt that short-nailed individuals are the "doers" of the world, not the "dreamers" or "spectators."

These nails are most often found among Square and Spatulate hands. Among these people, tension and frustration—often created by the people themselves—are more prevalent, and there are many "nail-biters" among owners of these fingernails. It shouldn't be surprising that, due to their heightened inner stress, these people tend to develop stomach problems as well.

Figure 27   *Figure 28*

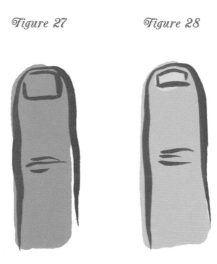

Figure 29   *Figure 30*

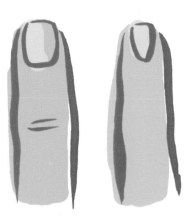

- People with a narrow lifestyle often find their parsimoniousness reflected in their extremely short and small fingernails (see Figure 28). If such nails are encountered on square-tipped fingers, such people are likely to lead dull, unadventurous lives.

- Nails that are as broad as they are long belong to people with practical and resource-ful personalities (see Figure 29). Since they're extremely dependable, honest, and loyal, they make excellent friends. These types of nails are encountered among many hand types, but rarely on Psychic/Intuitive hands, since they're most often characterized by long, almond-shaped nails.

- Dish-shaped nails are *not* a sign of robust health (see Figure 30, page 63). They may have taken on this shape after a shock or trauma, or it may be the result of continual tension. For instance, I have a friend with a congenital high-cholesterol condition whose nails are dish-shaped. Like other individuals with these nails, it's beneficial for her to avoid stressful situations whenever possible, and she needs to carefully watch her diet.

- Individuals with long, oval-shaped nails are generally less energetic than those with broad nails, but this doesn't indicate that they have poor health (see Figure 31). Since their disposition is very placid, the result is that they just don't use up as much energy as other types do. One of the characteristics inherent to such long, slender nails is patience with details, as well as with people—this would be a great asset in the teaching profession, in parenting, and in other related careers.

Figure 31

Figure 32

- Oval-shaped nails shouldn't be mistaken for those that are very narrow and tend to curl inward (see Figure 32). As you can see, fingernails such as these resemble the talons of birds of prey. People with such nails are egotistical and, not surprisingly, predatory by nature. They can spot opportunities that will benefit them with an "eagle eye."

The Color of Nails

Nails with a lively pink color are a sign of good health. If the color deepens to red, however, it reveals an agitated disposition that turns to anger at the slightest provocation.

Nails that are grayish or white reveal a lack of energy and vitality and are often a forewarning of health problems. If the nails have a bluish tint, it shows poor circulation.

The Texture of Nails

- Nails that are smooth, with semicircular "moons" showing at the base of the fingernails, are a sign of good health.

- Vertical ridges on fingernails suggest a nervous disposition; they can also form as a result of shock or trauma.

- If the nails are grooved horizontally, this points to a past infection or illness. Since it takes from six to nine months for the nail to grow out, one can estimate the time frame when the illness occurred.

- A similar situation is the presence of white specks in the fingernails—they may reveal a nervous disposition, or they may point to a time of stress or illness in the person's history. I myself have had these from time to time in my life. They indeed resulted from stressful situations and accurately pointed to the time when these conditions occurred. So, these specks are nothing to worry about. Providing that the person's health has improved, the specks will vanish when the nail grows out.

CHAPTER 6

The Mounts

*A*s you can see from Figure 33 on page 68, there are eight *mounts,* or elevated areas, on the palmar surface (indicated by the letters *A* through *H* on Figure 33). These mounts shouldn't be overlooked when analyzing a hand, as they show the distribution and flow of our energy.

Each mount is located under the finger of the same name. That is, the Mount of Jupiter *(C)* is located under the Jupiter finger; the Mount of Saturn *(D)* can be found beneath the Saturn finger; and the Mount of Apollo *(E)* appears at the base of the Apollo finger. But the thumb section has two mounts beneath it: (1) The

Figure 33

The Map of the Mounts

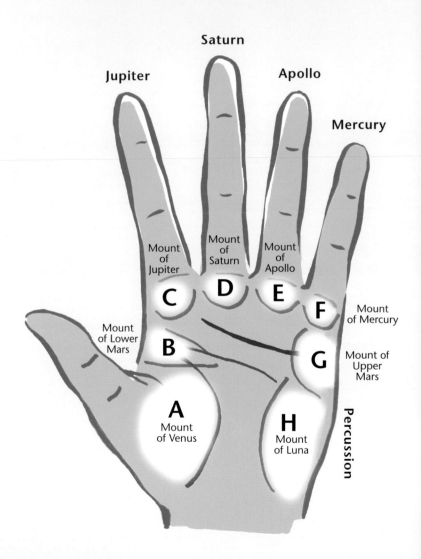

Saturn

Jupiter

Apollo

Mercury

Mount of Jupiter

Mount of Saturn

Mount of Apollo

C **D** **E** **F**

Mount of Mercury

Mount of Lower Mars

B **G**

Mount of Upper Mars

A
Mount of Venus

H
Mount of Luna

Percussion

large Mount of Venus *(A)*, which forms the root of the thumb and is encircled by the Life line (discussed in Chapter 8); and (2) the smaller, triangular Mount of Lower Mars *(B)*. In addition, the Mercury finger has three mounts located beneath it: (1) The Mount of Mercury *(F)*, located directly under the finger; (2) The Mount of Upper Mars *(G)*, situated beneath the Mount of Mercury *(F)*; and (3) the Mount of Luna *(H)*, which is at the very bottom. Thus, the mounts cover the entire hand— except for the center of the palm—forming a landscape of mountains and valleys.

Full or Flat Mounts

To judge whether the mounts are elevated or flat, the hand to be examined should be relaxed, with fingers bending slightly forward toward the palm. This will show the elevations and depressions more clearly. As a general rule, if the finger mounts are distinctive, the other mounts will follow suit. Yet there are many exceptions— a lack of development in one area and an enlargement in another may occur.

Fullness of the mounts reveals vitality and energy, but they also disclose a person's capacity for empathy and love—this is especially true regarding the Mounts of Venus and Apollo. But an exaggerated development doesn't increase the good qualities of a particular mount; rather, it detracts from it, since excess is never considered favorable in palmistry. For instance, if an exaggerated Mount of Venus is apparent, then this suggests that its owner is at the mercy of their own instincts and desires.

The Mount of Venus (A)

This mount lies in the Conscious, Passive half of the hand (which will be explained in the next chapter). The width and depth of this mount measures our capacity for love and sensuality, as well as for empathy and vitality. When small, flat, and hard, the individual is lacking these qualities. If the entire palm is thin and feels fleshless, resembling an arid wasteland, then that's an indication of diminished physical resources, especially if the skin color is pale.

The Mount of Lower Mars (B)

This mount is located directly above the Mount of Venus, and, if distinctive, points to physical courage and mental daring. A person with such a mount is likely to possess a fighting spirit, perseverance, and staying power, provided that the hand also has a strong thumb and favorable lines of Heart and Head (discussed in Chapter 8). But if the Mount of Lower Mars is excessively high and bulging, it suggests an aggressive nature—a person with this mount wouldn't need much encouragement to start a fight.

If the Mount of Lower Mars is flat or absent, a lack of courage or enterprise is indicated—such a person would take the passive approach to life. Absence of the Mount of Lower Mars is more common among the Psychic/Intuitive hand type, as these people are more yielding by nature; whereas the Square/Useful and Spatulate/Energetic types would be more likely to exhibit a mount that's rather prominent.

The Mount of Jupiter (C)

The Jupiter finger stands for ambition and achievement, so a well-padded mount increases the favorable qualities associated with it. A long, strong finger of Jupiter, with a developed mount, proclaims a desire to be in charge or command—but a finger of above-average length with a high mount would signify an excessive need for control; consequently, the person's leadership abilities would most likely turn to tyranny. Whether this person would apply physical force, or their need for control would take the shape of more intellectual ambitions, would largely depend on the type of hand they possess. People with the practical Square or the fiery Spatulate hand would have a greater inclination toward physical domination than the Philosophic/Intellectual, Psychic/Intuitive, or Conic/Artistic hand types, which would lean toward intellectual control.

The Mount of Saturn (D)

This finger forms the hypothetical division between the Conscious and Unconscious sectors of the palm (explained fully in the next chapter). If Saturn and its mount are proportioned well—neither too long nor too short, flat, or exaggerated—it reveals a good balance between the serious and lighthearted qualities of its owner. But if the finger is longer than average, coupled with an excessively high mount, this could be an indication of a morbid and somber nature. A shorter-than-average finger would indicate a disregard for law and order; together with a high mount, this might belong to someone with few scruples.

A flat or small mount can reveal disappointment in some area of a person's life: If encountered on the left hand only, this would point to a lack of enjoyment or problems in the personal life, whereas if found only on the right hand (assuming the person is right-handed), a depressed Mount of Saturn may reveal disappointment in his career. A lack of development in both hands, however, reveals sadness or a lack of enjoyment permeating the person's entire life.

The Mount of Apollo (E)

This mount is situated in the Unconscious zone of the hand. If it's distinctive, then this reflects an inborn appreciation of beauty and harmony, either as a lover of art and nature or in the realm of literature and poetry (this also applies to people with inborn social skills). Whether the person has chosen art as a hobby or as a career will be confirmed by the rest of their hand. For instance, someone with a career in the arts would most likely possess prominent Apollo and Fate lines (discussed in Chapter 9).

If the Apollo finger is longer than average—especially if it's coupled with an excessively high mount—it reveals a person's tendency toward gambling and extravagance. And if the mount is flat, with a shorter-than-average finger, such individuals probably get little enjoyment out of the beauty that surrounds them.

The Mount of Mercury (F)

This mount is situated in the Unconscious sphere of the hand, and it reveals our inclinations toward adventure and/or enterprise in every aspect of life. Since Mercury is the zone associated with communication in all areas, this also extends into intimate relationships.

A well-developed mount and a Mercury finger of at least average length shows a healthy appetite for excitement, love of travel, and so on, provided that the finger isn't bent or twisted. If this is the case, then the favorable qualities ascribed to the Mercury finger would be diminished, since a high mount together with a distorted finger would show a twisted or dishonest mentality. (Needless to say, such an assumption is invalid if a person's Mercury finger is bent, resulting from an arthritic condition or injury.)

The Mount of Upper Mars (G)

This mount lies directly below the Mount of Mercury, in the Unconscious zone of the hand, and it measures our passive and instinctive courage. The Mount of Upper Mars also reveals whether the ideas and daring promised by the Mount of Lower Mars are being realized. A flat or underdeveloped Upper Mars with a bulging Lower Mars would indicate that such a person is unlikely to have the staying power necessary to carry out their ideas; hence, they would tend to be critical and argumentative. If the Mount of Upper Mars is highly developed, then the outer edge of the hand (called the "Percussion") will be rounded or bulging, signifying resourcefulness and ingenuity.

The Mount of Luna (H)

This mount is situated across from the Mount of Venus and lies in the Unconscious/Instinctive zone of the hand. This sphere is associated with our creative imagination and is the nucleus of our entire personality, referred to as the "id." According to Freudian theory, the id consists of unconscious instincts and biological drives and is the foundation of an individual's personality.

A flat Mount of Luna would indicate a decrease of creativity and intuition—but if developed excessively, it could have even greater unfavorable ramifications. For instance, someone with an excessive Mount of Luna would tend to be unrealistic in their sentiments and ideas, which could lead to deviations—such as hero or cult worship—and if it's coupled with a very long Saturn finger, the person would lean toward having an imagination of a morbid nature.

As the mounts are strategically situated over the entire palmar surface, their development indicates where a person's energies are directed. This becomes even more significant as we move on to the divisions in the hand, which is the topic of the next chapter.

In the Palm of Your Hand

The Divisions in the Hand

hen examining a hand, consideration should first be given to its shape—and to the proportions between the palm, fingers, and thumb, which determines how each part relates to each other. Since we've covered this area in previous chapters, it's time to move on to the next step, which is to divide the palmar surface into vertical and horizontal sections. This is based on extensive study by many scholars and scientists. I obtained my knowledge from the works of Dr. Charlotte Wolff, a medical doctor who based her findings on past research and was vitally interested in discovering the temperament and character of a person from their hands. She developed her own psycho-physiological theory, based on the theory of *cerebral localization*, which translated to the different areas of the hand corresponding to various parts of a person's psyche.

The Vertical Division

The palm can be divided vertically into two hemi-spheres by drawing an imaginary line from the tip of the Saturn finger to the wrist (see Figure 34). This separates the palm into an Active/Outer zone and a Passive/Inner zone. This division coincides with the course of the two major nerves that bifurcate the hand: The section named for the *Ulnar* nerve veers from the Saturn finger to the outer edge of the hand (also called the "Percussion")— this is the *Passive Zone*. The *Radial* nerve follows in the direction of the Jupiter finger and the thumb—the section it forms is the *Active Zone*.

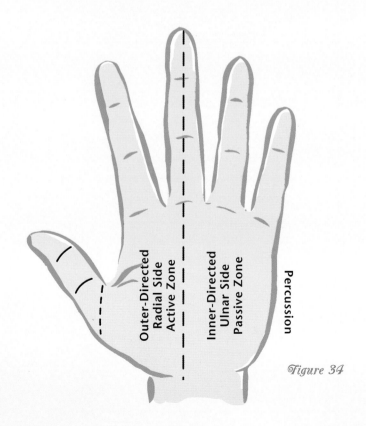

Outer-Directed
Radial Side
Active Zone

Inner-Directed
Ulnar Side
Passive Zone

Percussion

Figure 34

The Four Quadrants

Next, bisect the palm horizontally; this will segment the palm into four sections or quadrants (see Figure 35).

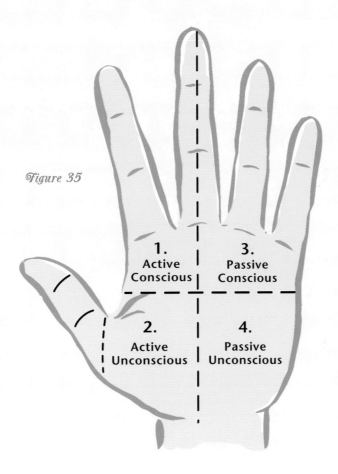

Figure 35

1.
Active
Conscious

3.
Passive
Conscious

2.
Active
Unconscious

4.
Passive
Unconscious

1. Active-Conscious

This includes the Jupiter finger, the top section of the thumb, and the Radial half of the Saturn finger. In the

Active-Conscious quadrant, the top part of the thumb represents our strength of will and the power of our endurance; the Jupiter finger, the Radial half of the Saturn finger, and their mounts point to our social attitudes and ambitions.

2. Active-Unconscious

In this zone, the sensuality and vitality ascribed to the Mount of Venus—found at the base of the thumb inside the Life line (see Figure 36, line *A*)—is combined with the aggressions and/or fighting spirit represented by the Mount of Lower Mars (located directly above the Mount of Venus). Since this quadrant lies in the Unconscious sphere of the hand, this is the area where people don't have full conscious control over their actions and reactions—here, behavior is dictated by one's individual character, moral values, and innate personality.

3. Passive-Conscious

This includes the fingers of Mercury and Apollo, and the Ulnar half of Saturn. The Passive-Conscious quadrant is associated with the inner-directed functions of our nature. Mercury is called "the messenger," and as such, points to all types of communication; Apollo is considered to be the "patron of the arts." The Saturn finger is divided into two halves, symbolizing our inner and outer demands and the ability to adapt to life's situations. Since Saturn is the most firmly rooted finger on the hand, it isn't as flexible as the other fingers. Should it lean toward

Jupiter, this would indicate an emphasis of outer-directed energies. But if it leans toward Apollo, then the energies are directed toward the Passive Zone—this hand's owner would tend to be cautious and introspective and have a greater need for emotional or material security.

4. Passive-Unconscious

This section includes the Upper Mount of Mars (located underneath the Mount of Mercury) and the Mount of Luna (found below the Upper Mount of Mars). As discussed in Chapter 8, the Mount of Luna contains our id, which is the seat of our creative imagination and it dictates our most instinctive behavior. Therefore, a well-developed Mount of Luna shows inborn creativity—and chances are, the mounts on the rest of the hand will confirm this.

The Mount of Upper Mars reveals whether the fighting spirit and daring promised by the Mount of Lower Mars (which is situated across the palmar surface) have been channeled into constructive endeavors. If both Mounts of Mars are distinctive, this signifies courage and perseverance; if only the Lower Mars is developed, this would indicate that the person hasn't been able to channel their mental daring into viable endeavors.

The Three Levels of Functioning

Finally, the palm is further divided horizontally—into three interrelating sections that represent all levels of functioning. The old masters used to divide the palm into two

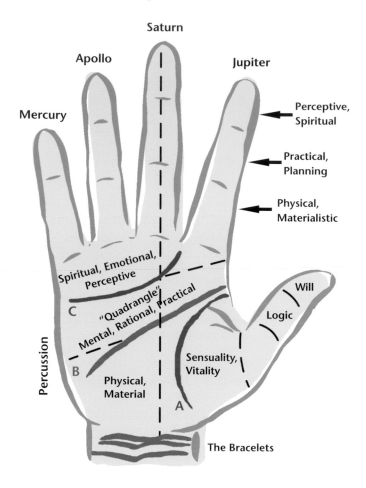

Figure 36

Saturn

Apollo

Jupiter

Mercury

Perceptive,
Spiritual

Practical,
Planning

Physical,
Materialistic

Spiritual, Emotional,
Perceptive

Will

C

"Quadrangle"

Logic

Mental, Rational, Practical

Percussion

B

Sensuality,
Vitality

Physical,
Material

A

The Bracelets

realms and had the fingers comprise a third; today, modern palmists divide not only the palm, but also the finger sections, into three separate yet connected spheres. These three levels represent our modes of functioning:

1. Spiritual/Emotional/Perceptive
2. Mental/Rational/Practical
3. Physical/Material

When examining a hand in this fashion, after studying the mounts and lines (which we'll get to in the next chapter), it becomes obvious where the person's flow of energy is directed. Any deviation from the "normal" or "average," such as exaggerations in a specific area, will point to the driving force of their personality. Contradictory indicators may manifest themselves in any of the three zones—these reveal ambivalence or idiosyncrasies and don't necessarily decrease a person's ability to function.

1. Spiritual/Emotional/Perceptive

The boundaries of this section lie between the Heart line (see Figure 36, line C) and the base of the fingers. It's a favorable sign if the Heart line is positioned high on the palm, for if it's placed low, encroaching on the area destined for the Head line (line *B*), this is an indication that the person's emotions tend to interfere with clear reasoning. Conversely, if the Head line is set high, trespassing on the space allowed for the Heart line, the owner of the hand could be ruthless and callous in their aims.

In the fingers, the first (nail) section refers to perceptive faculties. A long nail section, regardless of the hand type, reveals keen mental and/or spiritual perceptions. If encountered in the Jupiter finger, it relates to a person's leadership ability and their desire for responsibility or power. In the Saturn finger, a long first phalange reveals an inclination toward mysticism or religious fervor; if long and square-tipped, it expresses a high regard for law, order, and authority. If a long nail section is encountered in the Apollo finger, it's associated with artistic perceptions and ideas. In Mercury, a long first section reveals a gift for persuasion, which would be an excellent feature for public speakers, sales professionals, and actors.

2. Mental / Rational / Practical

The boundaries of this zone are the Head line, also called the "Line of Mentality," and the Heart line, which symbolizes our emotional makeup. This space, referred to as the "Quadrangle," measures our objectivity. Since the horizontal division of the hand splits it into two areas, that means that the section of the Quadrangle closest to the thumb (the Radial side) lies in the Conscious zone, while the outer edge of the palm (the Ulnar side) is in the Unconscious realm.

If the two major lines of Head and Heart are separated by a wide margin, then affairs of the heart wouldn't tend to interfere with the person's objective reasoning; a narrow space suggests the opposite.

In the fingers, the second (or middle) sections are associated with our practical abilities, but as the fingers reign over different areas of functioning, so do these sections have separate meanings. For instance, in the Jupiter finger, the second phalange measures a person's planning and executive abilities; in Saturn, this section relates to material values, practical abilities, and responsibility. In the Apollo finger, a long second section promises practical know-how in applying good taste or talents, as well as inborn social skills. The Mercury finger stands for all manners of communication, so here, the second phalange is associated with our daily modes of communication.

In the thumb, the second section is associated with the mental abilities of reasoning and logical deductions, whereas the tip refers to the will of the individual. Since the thumb is considered the most important finger of the hand, good proportions of the two sections are especially significant.

3. Physical/Material

The boundaries for this section are formed by the Head line and the lines at the wrist section, called "The Bracelets," which are clearly visible when bending the hand inward.

This entire section of the palm lies in the Unconscious zone and is associated with our physical and instinctual needs and appetites, which the Mount of Venus predicts. For instance, if this mount is fairly padded, yet firm, this points to vitality, personal warmth, and a healthy interest in sexuality for the hand's owner; if it's excessive or soft and flabby, such a person will most likely be at the mercy of their own impulses, rather than in control of them.

The seat of our deepest unconscious is the Mount of Luna—situated across from the Mount of Venus, under the Mercury finger. A prominent Mount of Luna should be accompanied by other signs of creativity or originality in the hand. These include: a long Apollo finger and developed Mount of Apollo; lines beneath Apollo (which will be discussed in Chapter 9); a Head line that curves slightly toward the Mount of Luna; and a rounded Percussion, which indicates resourcefulness and ingenuity.

In the fingers, the third or base section closest to the palm relates to our physical and instinctual desires. If this section dominates the other two phalanges in width or length, it may reveal charisma or a quest for physical power, especially if encountered in the Jupiter finger. An overly large third section of Saturn would emphasize a person's inclination toward traditional values. A long section in the Apollo finger reveals a discriminating taste in food, dress, or furnishings; if it's long and fat, such a person's taste would run toward quantity rather than quality. A long third section in the Mercury finger emphasizes independence in relationships.

These chapters have shown the physical aspect of the hand and fingers, and the distinct functions that each section is associated with. Part II will complete the picture by discussing the importance of the lines engraved upon the palmar surface.

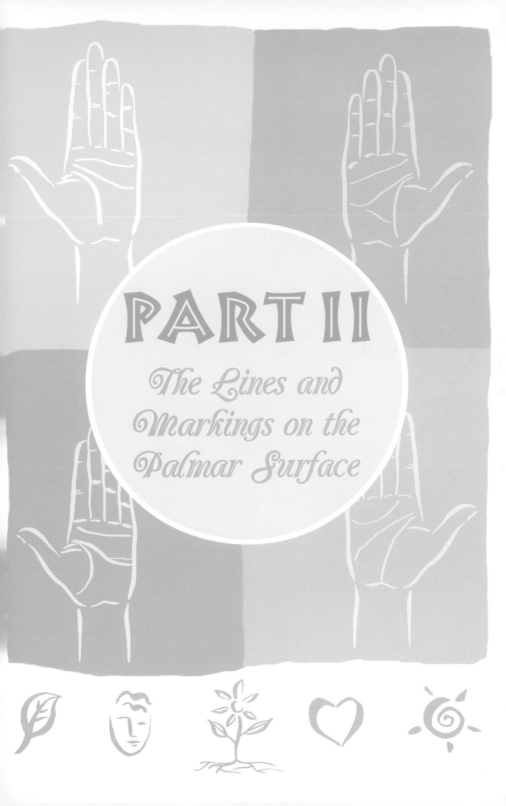

PART II

The Lines and Markings on the Palmar Surface

The Major Lines

*A*ll schools of palmistry consider the Life, Head, and Heart lines to be the major ones on the hand, since they're usually the most prominent and deep of all of the lines. Scientists have even proven that lines begin to appear in the hands of human embryos by the eighth week of life—the Life line comes first, followed by the Heart and then the Head lines.

It's of utmost importance to observe the starting and ending points of the major lines, especially since they vary so much from one hand to another, even on the same person.

CHAPTER 8

The Life Line

Most people associate this line with the length of life and invariably ask the same question: "How long will I live?" Although the Life line (see Figure 37, line *A*) is one of the lines from which an approximate time frame for a person's life can be obtained, it's a far greater yardstick for measuring their vitality and state of health than for predicting their longevity.

In most cases, the Life line starts at the edge of the hand, about midway between the insertion of the thumb

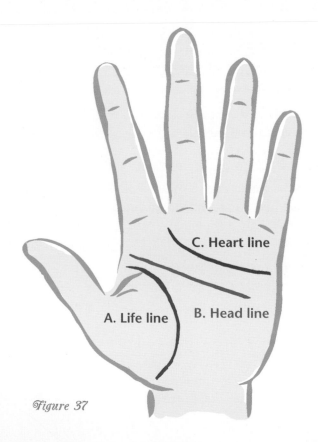

C. Heart line

A. Life line   **B. Head line**

Figure 37

and the Mount of Jupiter. If this line has a chained or weak beginning, or if the line is barely visible at this point, then there may have been physical difficulties at the time of birth; as the child gets older and stronger, the Life line will reflect this positive change.

If the Life line forms a wide circle around the Mount of Venus, this is indicative of someone with an adventurous nature and an extroverted personality—or someone who at least prefers variety to monotony. But if the Life line hugs the thumb closely and forms a narrow path around the Mount of Venus, this implies that the individual is timid and cautious.

Color and Depth

If the color of the Life line is a healthy pink, and the line itself is clearly marked, this is a sign of vitality, as well as of physical and psychological stamina; but if the color deepens to dark red, this points to an agitated and aggressive temperament.

If the line is deep (but not trenchlike), it probably belongs to someone with strong feelings and attitudes who's been blessed with inborn endurance and energy. Once someone like this is set on a course, they'll rarely change it.

If the Life line is thin, fragile, marked with dots or islands, or has spiderweb-like lines descending from it, then the opposite holds true: This person will tend to lack vitality, often due to diminished physical energy.

The Second Life Line

Occasionally, a hand will show two distinct Life lines running in separate directions. This suggests that its owner leads two different lives. An example of this would be the actor—whose professional life is "public property"—who is actually a recluse at heart and who would do anything to screen their private domain from observation.

Forks on the Life Line

If there are distinct branches veering off in other directions from the Life line, it gives an added dimension to the individual's personality. The direction of the fork indicates the area where the person's energy is going.

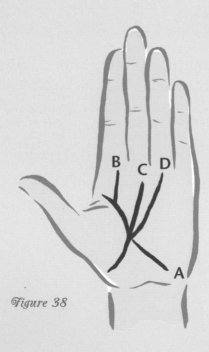

Figure 38

- If the branch is directed toward the **Mount of Luna** (see Figure 38, letter *A*), owners of this hand tend to like travel and adventure, but if the main line continues its course around the thumb, it reveals that they also treasure their home and family.

- A branch from the Life line to the **Mount of Jupiter** (see Figure 38, letter *B*) signifies aspirations and a desire for leadership—it's also referred to as the "Ambition line." The stronger this branch is, and the closer it reaches to its destination of the Mount of Jupiter, the better a person's chances are of realizing their goals.

- If a branch line is directed toward the **Mount of Saturn** (see Figure 38, letter *C*), it's also called the "Effort line." If this is present, then the person's success will most likely not be handed to them—they'll achieve through their *own* endeavors.

- A branch in the direction of the **Mount of Apollo** (see Figure 38, letter *D*) is called the "Success line," but as is the case with the Effort line, such accomplishment will tend to be achieved through the person's own effort. As the saying goes, "We make our own luck."

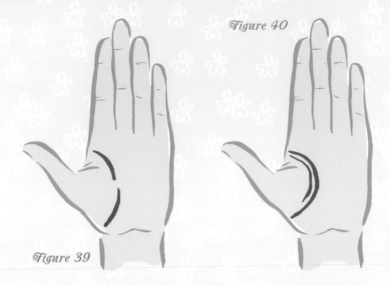

Figure 40

Figure 39

Interruptions of the Life Line

If the Life line is interrupted at some point during its course—but continues after the break, with a new line forming between the two ends—this indicates a change in the person's lifestyle (see Figure 39). If the line after the interruption is stronger or forms a wider circle than it did before, then the change will have been favorable. But if the Life line is weaker after the break or hugs the thumb in a closer circle, then the opposite holds true.

The Influence Line

If a thinner, parallel line accompanies the Life line on the inside, it's called the "Influence line" (see Figure 40). If a hand has an Influence line, this is a favorable sign, since it enhances nature's resistance to illness and infections. This person is likely to possess a very healthy immune system.

The Head Line

This is also referred to as the "Line of Mentality" and is considered to be the second most important line on the hand (see Figure 37, line *B,* page 88).

The Head line—as indicated by its length, smoothness, and starting and ending points—gives a clue to the person's reasoning and mental capacity. It's very important that this line be relatively free of additional markings, such as islands, dots, crosses, or fine hairlines descending from it. (The meaning of such markings will be discussed later in this chapter.)

As for the color and depth of the line, the same characteristics apply as for the Life line—that is, if it's pink and clearly marked, this is a sign of vitality and physical and psychological stamina. And just like the Life line, the Head line should be deep, but not overly so.

Both hands of a person must be examined in order to compare possible differences between the birth and dominant hands. For example, let's say that we're examining the hands of a right-handed person, and the Head line in their right (dominant) hand is longer and straighter, or with additional forks, than their left (birth) hand—this is an indication that the person has come far in developing their potential. This finding would be confirmed if the person's dominant hand also had a longer Fate line, the presence of Effort or Success lines, a strong thumb, good development of the Mounts, and/or balanced proportions between the fingers and palm.

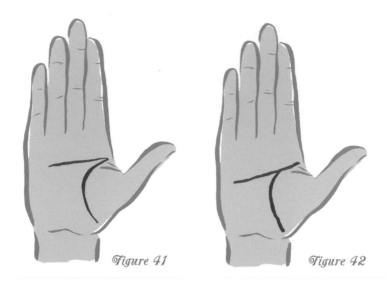

Figure 41 *Figure 42*

The Starting Points

These reveal a person's inborn attitudes and tendencies at a glance.

- People who possess a Head line that starts with their Life line (see Figure 41) and touches it at its inception are cautious by nature and moderate in their lifestyle. They have a tendency to uphold traditions and seldom go to extremes in anything; they're also neither excessively aggressive nor gullible.

- If the lines of Life and Head are tightly meshed at the beginning (see Figure 42) and follow the same course for a distance, this reveals more-than-average caution. Such people would tend to be extremely sensitive about receiving criticism and about what others feel and think about them. Since this often reflects an inherent lack of self-confidence, these people would not be inclined to handle failure very well.

- If the Head line starts inside the Life line, from the Mount of Lower Mars (see Figure 43), then the characteristics mentioned above would be enhanced, coupled with the excitability and aggressiveness ascribed to the Mount of Lower Mars. It should be obvious that such a starting point for the Head line isn't favorable, but if this line follows a straight course across the palm, after emerging from within the Mount of Lower Mars, it does indicate that the person has overcome unfavorable tendencies and has added a measure of common sense and self-control to their personality.

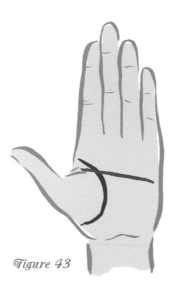

Figure 43

- If the Head line displays a weakness after beginning inside the Life line, or if it continues in an excessively declining course toward the center of the palm (see Figure 44), then this suggests that the person hasn't been able to overcome the unfavorable characteristics associated with the line's beginning.

Keep in mind that each one of us starts out in life with positive and negative genetic tendencies—some people are able to overcome tough breaks in life, while others who have been born with all of life's advantages end up sabotaging their chances. There are no easy answers for why this happens, and unfortunately, palms hold no clues to these intriguing puzzles.

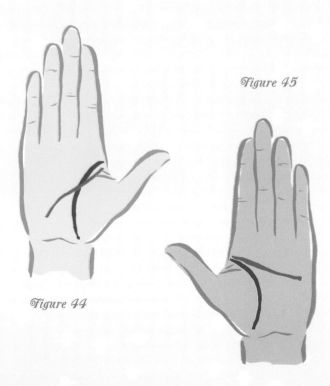

Figure 45

Figure 44

- If the Head line is separated from the Life line by a small margin (see Figure 45), self-reliance and independent thought are revealed. These people don't tend to find it difficult to make decisions; it shouldn't be surprising that they're born leaders.

- If the space between the Head and Life lines is wide (see Figure 46), this does *not* mean that the above qualities are enhanced. Quickness in decision-making may turn into rashness and impulsiveness, and courage could become recklessness. These people would benefit from possessing a strong thumb as a balance, for such a wide separation of the two major lines at the starting point, coupled with an excessively flexible thumb, would enhance their impulsive tendencies.

Figure 46

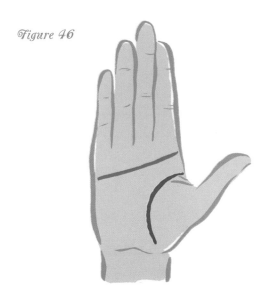

The Course of the Head Line

According to Cheiro, it's of utmost significance to realize that the course of the Head line should be different in the various hand types; after all, what's normal for the Square hand would be unusual in the Psychic/Intuitive type. For instance, on the Square hand, a straight course of the Head line is normal—if it should slant toward the Mount of Luna, then a degree of versatility and creative imagination are added to its primarily materialistic and practical personality. But if the line slants excessively, terminating on the Mount of Luna itself, this wouldn't be a favorable position for the Square hand type; since they're not known for being too insightful or philosophic, these people would be at the mercy of depression.

- A Head line that lies across the palm from the starting point to the Percussion (see Figure 48, page 100) is considered long, since the average line stops beneath the Mount of Apollo. Such a lengthy, straight line is indicative of someone who has chosen a practical and materialistic course in life and knows exactly how to go about achieving their aims. This can also be indicative of a somewhat egotistical nature. If the line were to have a small fork in the direction of the Mount of Luna, this would be favorable, since it would add creative imagination of a rather disciplined nature.

- The straight, deep Head line shows practicality with good common sense. Someone with this line wouldn't be easily sidetracked into many different ventures, but would have the ability to concentrate their efforts on any given task or project. This type of Head line is most often encountered in the Square/Useful hand, yet it certainly does not signify diminished mental capacity. Rather, it shows concentration and a single-mindedness of purpose. I've observed such short, deep Head lines on people with a very keen mentality. A straight line *without* unfavorable markings—such as dots, crosses, or islands—is more favorable than a long line *with* them.

- As mentioned above, a gently curving Head line is normal when it belongs to the Psychic/Intuitive hand and, to a lesser degree, the Conic/Artistic type. Yet, a line that slants excessively, terminating on the Mount of Luna itself, or one that ends near the wrist after separation from the Life line, is considered abnormal. This reflects a somber or morbid outlook on life, and possibly suicidal tendencies. This kind of position of the Head line needs a strong thumb to balance it.

Forks on the Head Line

Forks on the Head line add an extra dimension to a person's mentality.

- A fork at the end of a long, slightly curving Head line (see Figure 47, page 100) reveals the gift of self-expression, both verbally and through the written word. This is referred to as the "Writer's Fork," and if coupled with a long Apollo finger, it's almost certain that such an individual possesses a talent for writing.

Such people also have an inborn understanding of human nature, which allows them to see both sides of a story or problem. This ability would be an asset for many professions, from the psychologist to the social worker; but it would especially benefit actors, since they would have the capability to immerse themselves into the characters they portray.

- As mentioned on page 98, a very long, straight Head line (see Figure 48) would benefit from having a fork directed toward the Mount of Luna, for this would indicate a greater understanding of human nature.

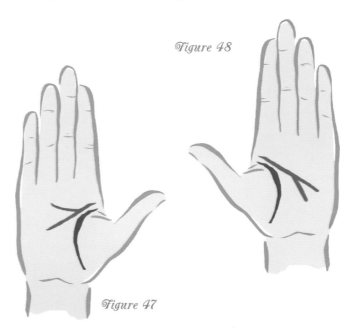

Figure 48

Figure 47

Figure 50

Figure 49

- A fork branching toward the Mount of Mercury (see Figure 49)—the sphere of expression and communication—is also referred to as the "Lawyer's Fork," since people of this profession tend to have a facility for verbal expression and are known for their ability to debate. This would also be an asset on a politician's hand.

- A three-pronged fork (see Figure 50), with a straight main line branching toward the Mounts of Mercury and Luna, indicates versatility and suggests a keen, multidimensional intelligence. Such a person is endowed with common sense, as well as creative imagination.

- A Head line divided into two large forks (see Figure 51) is not as favorable, for this reflects a "split" personality, one that would find it difficult to make decisions or concentrate on one course in life.

The Wavy Head Line

- A wavy Head line (see Figure 52), coupled with changes in the line's depth, reveals uncertainty in the person's intellectual life.

- An interrupted Head line, with an Influence line connecting the two ends (see Figure 53), may be indicative of a trauma affecting the brain. The Influence line is a sign of recovery, provided that the line continues smoothly after the break.

Figure 51

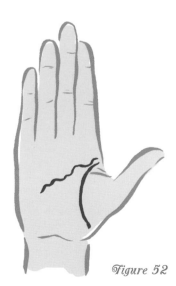

Figure 52

- A frayed Head line (see Figure 54), or a Head line coupled with an island (see Figure 55), shows feeblemindedness and a lack of logical thought processes. This may be encountered in the hands of mentally retarded people, or in those with impaired concentration and learning abilities. In severe cases, such a Head line would be accompanied by a short or deformed thumb.

Figure 53

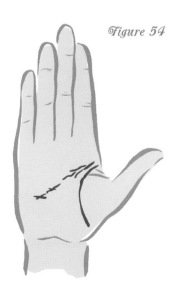

Figure 54

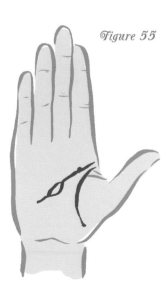

Figure 55

The Heart Line

The *course* of this line reveals our emotional makeup, but the line itself (see Figure 37, line C, page 88), with regard to depth, color, and smoothness, deals primarily with our physical health.

The Starting Points

- A Heart line starting from the Mount of Jupiter (see Figure 56) shows loyalty and reliability regarding affections. Such people would tend to have very high standards and expectations when it comes to the ones they love.

  A line beginning from the finger of Jupiter itself, however, suggests that these people could be blind to the faults of those they worship, which is bound to result in disappointments later on.

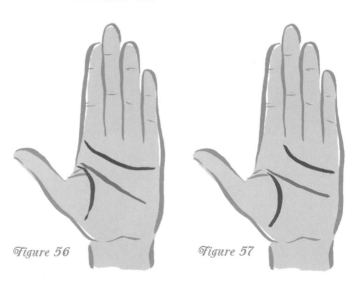

Figure 56   *Figure 57*

- A Heart line that starts between and below the fingers of Jupiter and Saturn (see Figure 57), reveals deep feelings, but it also points to a calm disposition relating to the affections— falling somewhere between the idealism of Jupiter and the passion of Saturn.

- If the Heart line rises from the Mount of Saturn (see Figure 58), then such a person would be seen to have a passionate, yet selfish, nature. Their primary interest would be focused on their own desires and needs. These characteristics are further enhanced if the Heart line rises from the Saturn finger itself.

- A Heart line that covers the entire palm from side to side (see Figure 59) is considered excessively long and shows an exaggerated need for attention and a tendency toward jealousy.

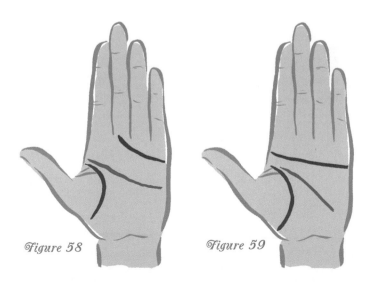

Figure 58   *Figure 59*

The Positions of the Heart Line

Remember that the space between the Head and Heart lines is called "the Quadrangle" (see Figure 36, page 80). It reveals how a person deals with affairs of the heart and head, and also shows how objective they can be. The Head and Heart lines shouldn't infringe on each other's territories.

- If the Heart line lies low on the palm (see Figure 60) and approaches the territory of the Head line, narrowing the Quadrangle, a person's objective reasoning may be jeopardized by their feelings.

- If the Head line encroaches upon the space destined for the Heart line (see Figure 61), this indicates that the person is heartless and calculating. Someone with this positioning may have a tendency toward premeditated crimes.

Figure 60

Figure 61   *Figure 62*

In his book *Language of the Hand*, Cheiro describes a case from the early 1930s, in which a doctor in Chicago murdered many of his wealthy clients after persuading them to sign over their life insurance policies to him. The doctor was finally caught, and rather famously put on trial.

Cheiro was shown the doctor's handprints and correctly interpreted them: He told the authorities that while the accused's left (birth) hand showed nothing unusual (it revealed intelligence and even altruism), his right (dominant) hand indicated criminal tendencies, judged by a Head line that practically swallowed up the Heart line (see Figure 62).

The Quality of the Heart Line

As with all lines, smoothness and a light pink color on the Heart line indicate good health. If many hairline branches, called "capillary lines," descend from or ascend to the Heart line, this points to a flirtatious nature; if the main line is heavily frayed, then this would reveal potential or existing health problems involving the organ itself, such as high cholesterol or elevated blood pressure.

A broad and chained Heart line beginning from Saturn reflects contempt for the opposite sex. If the Heart line is pale and broad, this signifies indifference; conversely, if the line is bright red, this indicates extreme passion or agitation, with a temper to match.

Islands, dots, and interruptions on the Heart line represent obstacles, which point to potential or existing health problems.

The Simian Line

As already mentioned, if the lines of Heart and Head are fused together into one, it's referred to as "the Simian line." As the name implies, the fusion of these two principal lines is primarily found in the hands of apes and monkeys, as is clearly evident in the hand of an orangutan (see Figure 15, page 48).

If only sections of the lines are joined (see Figure 63), or if there's an Influence line connecting the two lines (see Figure 64), then this is considered a *partial* Simian line.

If the Simian line is present in human hands, it shouldn't automatically be judged as a sign of low mentality. In fact, some palmists insist that it's a sure indication of genius. It's important to observe which hand the line appears in. It may even appear in both hands; if this is the case, then the person will tend to pursue their goals and objectives with a dogged single-mindedness, which may work positively for individuals whose efforts are directed into creative endeavors.

In hands with many negative characteristics, such as a weak thumb, or an exaggerated development of the Mounts of Venus and Lower Mars, the Simian line isn't considered favorable. Such a person would tend to be at the mercy of their own impulses and would lack sound judgment.

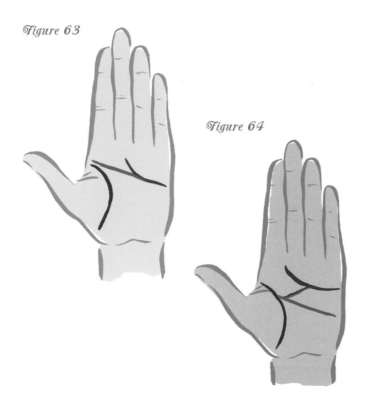

Figure 63

Figure 64

Other Markings on the Palm

These markings have special significance when appearing on the Life, Head, or Heart lines, but they may also appear in other areas of the palm, such as on the mounts and in the center of the hand. Palmists assert that these markings are manifestations of our central nervous system and are subject to change, or will fade out when the person's health has improved.

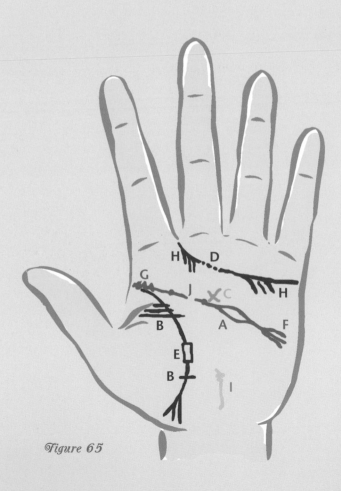

Figure 65

Islands

Islands (see Figure 65, letter *A*) on any line are an unfavorable sign, but they're especially negative if present on the major lines, for this reveals weakness in potential or existing health problems. However, if the line continues smoothly after the island, health will have been restored.

On the Heart line, an island refers to physical difficulties that affect that organ, rather than to a "broken heart." On the Head line, an island points to trauma or injury to the head or brain—the result would be a lack of logical thought processes or concentration for the duration of such an island. On the Life line, an island shows temporary difficulties or problems of a physical or emotional nature.

Horizontal Bars

Any horizontal markings (see Figure 65, letter *B*) are obstacles and/or interferences upon the line, which decrease its favorable qualities. As always, these bars are most detrimental if encountered on one of the major lines, but it will depend on how or if the line continues on after a crossing bar.

Other horizontal markings are the worry lines, most often exhibited on the Mounts of Venus and Lower Mars. They reveal a highly sensitive disposition that's given to worrying excessively and often needlessly.

Crosses

Crosses are two lines that intersect each other (see Figure 65, letter C) and for the most part, are unfavorable markings. When found on a major line, they show difficulties and hindrances related to the specific area where they're encountered.

There are only two places where a cross can be interpreted favorably: (1) In the Quadrangle, positioned between the Head and Heart lines; and (2) on the Mount of Jupiter. The first is referred to as "the Mystic Cross" and reflects a high degree of intuitive faculties in those who possess it. Intuition is further enhanced if encountered in the Psychic/Intuitive hand. The second points to leadership abilities, provided that the finger of Jupiter is straight and of at least average length.

Broken Lines

Broken lines (see Figure 65, letter D) are never favorable, but if the ends are connected by an Influence line, it promises recovery. For instance, as I've already mentioned, breaks in the Head line indicate a disruption of logical thought processes and a lack of concentration, but if an Influence line connects both ends of the lines, this is a sign that normal functioning of the brain has been restored. An Influence line shouldn't be confused with a double Head line, where two lines run separate courses. A double Head line points to versatility and tends to belong to people with multifaceted personalities—in fact, the hands of Cheiro showed such a marking (see page 226)—but it's a relatively rare occurrence.

Squares

This is a favorable marking, since squares on any line (see Figure 65, letter *E*) are a sign of protection. On the Head line, squares reveal ingenuity and resourcefulness; on the Life and Heart lines, they guard against illness or injury.

Tassels and Frayed Lines

Any line that is frayed or ends in a tassel (see Figure 65, letter *F*) is a sign of weakness and diminished energy. On the Life line, this marking is generally seen at the end of the line near the wrist, indicating an ebbing of the life forces. Yet, frayed lines can occur at any point on any line, but as always, they're especially significant and unfavorable if present on one of the major lines.

Chained Formations

These are often present at the beginning of a line, such as at the starting point of the Life and Head lines (see Figure 65, letter *G*). If the lines continue smoothly on afterward, this is a sign that obstacles or difficulties have been conquered or removed. Most palmists agree that chained formations on the Heart line refer to a heart as an organ, *not* to the affections. Chained formations—as well as dots, crosses, or islands—reveal tendencies or existing physical problems involving the heart. If found on the Head line (other than at the beginning point), this shows a lack of concentration and/or clear thinking processes, which would be considered a weakness involving the intellect.

Capillary Lines

These are fine lines that either ascend to or descend from the main lines (see Figure 65, letter *H*); rising lines are said to be more favorable, as they show an upward direction. Capillary lines are thinner at the ends, which is one way to ascertain whether they're ascending or descending. Like chained formations, capillary lines are considered a sign of weakness. If the entire palm is covered by a network of such "spider web" lines running aimlessly in all directions, this indicates a highly nervous temperament and may reflect severe mental distress or chronic anxiety.

Wavy Lines

(See Figure 65, letter *I*.) A wavy Head line shows a lack of concentration or clear goals—if found in a student's hand, it's certain that they're very easily distracted. A wavy Heart line gives a clue to a fickle nature concerning the person's emotions and affections. A wavy Fate line (discussed in the next chapter) reveals ambivalence in someone's outlook on life and/or uncertainty in their career.

Dots

Dots on any of the lines (see Figure 65, letter *J*) indicate temporary difficulties in the areas where they occur. Since they tend to make their appearance when difficulties arise, such as during times of illness or excessive stress, dots may disappear or fade out when health has been restored, which is also the case with the other markings. Dots are not nearly as permanent as the other markings are.

The Minor Lines

The Fate Line

Most palmists agree that the Fate line is just about the most important minor line on the hand. It's especially significant because not every palm has one.

In her book *The Human Hand,* Dr. Charlotte Wolff explains that the Fate line is a *crease line,* as are the major lines of Life, Head, and Heart. She writes that the complete absence of accessory crease lines, even in the Elementary hand, signifies a person's lack of sensitivity, while an abundance of them indicates a high degree of receptiveness. If you bend your fingers inward by half-closing your hand, you'll reveal your own palm's crease lines—if you have a Fate line, it will be folded or creased vertically.

CHAPTER 9

The Fate line is alternately called the "Line of Destiny" or "Career line." It's also been named the "Line of Adaptability," which I feel describes this line particularly well, since those who possess a Fate line seem to strive to adapt their inner self to the demands of the outer world, and by doing so tend to develop a strong philosophy to meet their goals.

According to Cheiro, it's important to observe what type of hand the Fate line exists on, for he felt that it's more frequently seen among the Philosophic, Conic, and Psychic hand types than in the Square or Spatulate hands. Cheiro's explanation for this was that people whose hands fall into the former categories are by nature more attuned to philosophic and theoretical idealism than the other two types—whose first and foremost aim is to translate their knowledge and endeavors into practical and viable solutions. Therefore, if the Fate line is present on a Practical or Spatulate hand, it's even more worthy of notice, since this line adds insight and understanding of human nature for those who possess it.

The closer the line gets to its destination of the Mount of Saturn, the stronger the person's philosophy of life and their efforts toward self-realization would be.

Figure 66

Starting and Ending Positions

- If the line starts low in the hand—that is, from or near the wrist (see Figure 66)—this suggests that the person has set their goals early in life. Such a starting point also reveals highly developed social instincts.

  If the Fate line continues upward into the palm, but stops at the Head line, this individual wouldn't tend to set new goals or challenges for themselves after the age of 30 or 35. They may be completely satisfied with their career or personal life and just aren't contemplating any new directions, or this can be a sign of stagnation. (This analysis wouldn't apply if the person has yet to reach the age of 30, for the line may extend with growing years.)

- If the line continues past the Head line (see Figure 67), this symbolizes untiring efforts toward reaching new avenues.

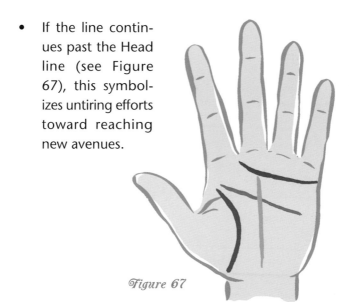

Figure 67

- If the Fate line starts higher in the palm (see Figure 68), it indicates that the individual's career or personal goals weren't set early; they most likely "came into their own" later in life.

- Another starting point is from the Life line itself (see Figure 69). If the Fate and Life lines are tied together, then the person's family has probably had a strong influence in their early years . . . which can have a positive *or* negative effect.

  If the Fate line starts from the Mount of Venus, crosses the Life line, and continues on its course toward the Mount of Saturn (see Figure 69, line *A*), or if a branch of the Fate line is directed toward the Mounts of Apollo or Mercury (see Figure 69, line *B*), this may signify an inborn talent that runs in the family, such as a propensity toward music or the arts.

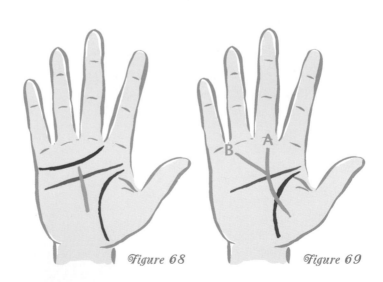

Figure 68   *Figure 69*

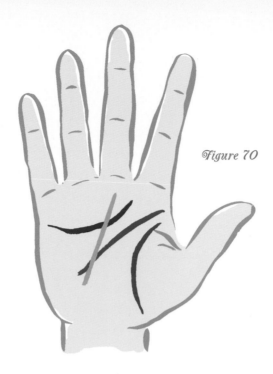

Figure 70

- A Fate line that starts from the Mount of Luna (see Figure 70) reveals strong influences from outside the confines of the family. This person's career or success may have been assisted by other individuals who helped catapult them into the limelight. This is usually the case with actors or politicians, for they're more often than not aided by influential friends and/or romantic partners.

Branches of the Fate Line

- If a branch from the Fate line follows in the direction of the Mount of Jupiter (see Figure 71, line *A*, page 122), this signifies that a per-

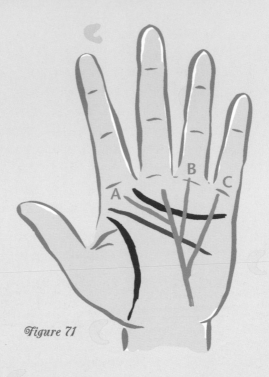

Figure 71

son's efforts and ambitions have been channeled into careers and leadership, where they would have the opportunity to take responsibility for others. This desire is especially enhanced by a long, strong Jupiter finger.

- A branch line toward the Mount of Apollo (see Figure 71, line *B*) indicates that the individual's efforts would be directed toward creative endeavors, or it may indicate a strong desire for personal happiness and a harmonious existence.

- Since the Mount of Mercury is associated with communication and expression in all areas, a branch from the Fate line to this mount (see Figure 71, line C) points to an individual's proficiency in the fields of science, business, music, and the arts. Mercury is also known as "the finger of enterprise," so a long Mercury finger would further enhance their chances for success.

The Sister Line

If a second line (see Figure 72) accompanies the Fate line during part of its course, this is called a "Sister line." A Sister line tends to be a sign of strength, but if it becomes stronger than the main line, or if it has branches that veer off to any of the mounts, then it will have become dominant over the Fate line.

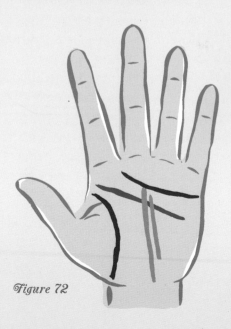

Figure 72

Other Markings

Markings on the Fate line, such as dots, crosses, islands, bars, interruptions, or waves aren't seen as favorable (squares are the exception), for they detract from the positive qualities attributed to the Fate line. It's debatable whether a Fate line with negative markings (which symbolize obstacles) is more or less favorable than the absence of the line itself. Is it better to have tried and failed at something, or to not have tried at all? I leave this eternal question for my readers to answer. . . .

The Apollo Line

The Apollo line, alternately referred to as the "Sun line," "the Line of Brilliance," or "the Success line," isn't an uncommon line to possess. It indicates good social skills and promises success and brilliance (as the various names for it imply)—but these qualities are as much a reflection of personal fulfillment, resourcefulness, and adaptability as they are a yardstick of "outer" success.

As with the Fate line, it's important to observe the type of hand that the Apollo line appears on, as it's most often found among the Conic/Artistic, Philosophic, or Psychic hand types. If it appears on Square or Spatulate hands, it takes on an even greater significance—here, its influence might manifest as an increased creativity or a sunny nature.

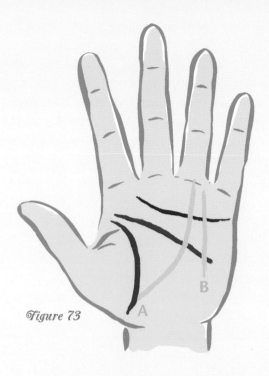

Figure 73

The Starting Positions

The Apollo line may originate from the Life, Head, or Heart lines, or from the Mount of Luna. Although its starting points are varied, the destination is the same: on or near the Mount of Apollo.

- If the line starts from the Life line (see Figure 73, line A), close to the wrist, this suggests that the person is a great lover of beauty or has even devoted their entire life to the arts. Such an individual would be born with a refined taste in clothing, furnishings, and the art of living.

Other features on the hand—such as a strong branch from the Fate line toward the Apollo finger, a curving Head line (possibly forked toward the direction of the Mount of Luna), and/or a long finger and highly developed Mount of Apollo—would give clues as to whether or not a career has resulted from having this early starting position.

- If the Apollo line is present in a hand with a Head line that slants toward the Mount of Luna, creative imagination is revealed, so success or talent is more likely to occur in the field of literature or poetry.

  If the Apollo line starts from the Mount of Luna (see Figure 73, line *B,* page 125), this points to a career or interest in politics or the stage, since such a starting position suggests a greater dependence on the whims or influence of others.

- If the Apollo line rises from or close to the Head line (see Figure 74, line *A*), success will tend to occur due to the individual's own efforts, but it's likely to happen later in life.

- An Apollo line that starts from the Heart line (see Figure 74, line *B*) indicates good taste and an appreciation of beauty. This starting point may reveal a second career that involves creative endeavors, in any area. Multiple lines indicate a variety of interests, but they'd probably be too diverse to apply to a single career.

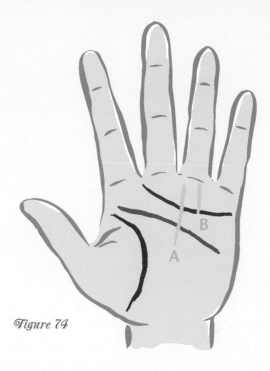

Figure 74

The Mercury Line

Palmists don't totally agree when it comes to interpreting this line, which is also referred to as the "Line of Health." But generally speaking, a person with this line wouldn't tend to rely on logical deductions alone, for they're endowed with inborn understanding and insight—the stronger the line, the greater the gift of this "sixth sense." For instance, if the Mercury line was found on the hand of a doctor or nurse, this would indicate that they're an excellent diagnostician.

According to Cheiro, this line rises from the Mount of Mercury and not from the palm (see Figure 75, line C, page 129), as the other lines do. He maintained that the presence of the Mercury line is evidence of robust health.

However, it should never become stronger than a major line, or cross the Life line, for this would be an indication of illness or death. I must caution anyone reading hands not to make such predictions, since the power of pessimistic suggestions can be so strong that such a proclamation could have a severe negative impact.

Other Lines on the Hand

The Girdle of Venus

This is a semicircular line that swings between the fingers of Jupiter and Mercury (see Figure 75, line A). Because it takes its name from the goddess of love, some palmists have ascribed an overabundance of sensuality to the Girdle of Venus. According to Cheiro, this is an exaggerated assumption, since this line is located in the Conscious part of the hand (see page 77) and corresponds to our Mental/Perceptive brain activities. Therefore, the characteristics of the *Girdle* of Venus aren't the same as those attributed to the *Mount* of Venus. Because the Mount is located in the lower half of the hand, it relates to our instinctive, hormonal needs and desires.

Cheiro felt that people who possess the Girdle of Venus are more apt to dream and fantasize about sensual experiences. They also tend to be sensitive, receptive to outside stimuli, and subject to mood swings, especially if the Girdle is fragmented into pieces. If the Girdle is reinforced by one or more parallel lines, the desire for adventure and/or preoccupation with sexual fantasies would be intensified. Someone with this formation would benefit from having a firmly rooted thumb as a balance.

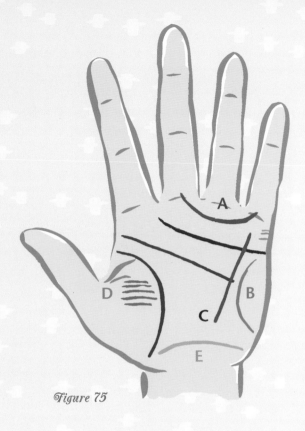

Figure 75

The Intuition Crescent

This line forms a semicircular path from the face of the Mount of Mercury to the Mount of Luna (see Figure 75, line *B*), or it may be seen on the Mount of Luna alone.

The Intuition Crescent is easier to observe if the hand is relaxed, with fingers bent inward. The line appears more frequently among the Philosophic, Conic, and Psychic hand types, but isn't restricted to these categories. If encountered on Square or Spatulate hands, the line adds shrewdness and an instinctive business acumen to these people's common sense. Such individuals can "smell a bargain" or a good deal instantly. Wherever this line is found, it reveals insight, which may be coupled with a gift of presentiment or clairvoyance in various degrees.

(This marking shouldn't be confused with the line of Mercury [see Figure 75, line C, page 129], even though they're both located in the same proximity and might even cross each other.)

Worry Lines

Horizontal lines inside the Life line, on the Mount of Venus, are called Worry Lines (see Figure 75, line D, page 129). If they intersect the Life line, then this points to the type of temperament that tends to fret needlessly—in which case, the entire palm may also be crisscrossed with fine lines.

Via Lasciva or Poison Line

This semicircular line is found near the wrist, connecting the Mount of Luna with that of Venus (see Figure 75, line E, page 129). A variation of the Poison line is a line that curves to the wrist from the Mount of Luna, without connecting to the Mount of Venus.

The name given to this line is taken from the Latin and translates as "lascivious." According to Cheiro and other palmists, the line is associated with unchecked sensuality and passion. If it cuts the Life line, this would be interpreted as "death by overindulgence," be it in the form of food, alcohol, or other substances.

The alternate name given to this line—"Poison line"— suggests that the person would tend to react adversely to certain drugs, alcohol, or food. I have an excellent example of such a Poison line from my collection (seen in Figure 113, page 205). The hand belongs to a 57-year-old man who is highly allergic to lobster meat. He has very strong reactions to even the tiniest portion of it, and is further unable to tolerate general anesthesia due to the drugs used in this process. So, I feel that the existence of this line is a far greater indication of a person's physical tendencies, such as allergies, rather than of their lifestyle.

Marriage and Relationship Lines

These are horizontal markings on the Mount of Mercury, on the outer edge of the hand (see Figure 76), and their presence reflects a person's ability to engage in a committed, give-and-take relationship with another person (it doesn't necessarily have to be marriage). The stronger and deeper the Marriage and Relationship lines are, the greater and more lasting their influence is.

Figure 76

- If a Marriage line lies close to the Heart line, this signifies a serious relationship early in life, usually from about 14 to 21 years of age.

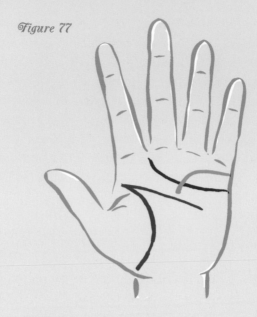

Figure 77

- If the line is situated between the Heart line and the base of the Mercury finger, the time frame for the significant relationship would most likely be between 21 and 28 years.

- A Marriage line that's closer to the base of the fingers suggests a meaningful relationship that will happen in the latter part of a person's life.

- Marriage and Relationship lines that end in a descending curve (see Figure 77)—or those with islands, dots, or horizontal bars—reflect a troubled relationship.

- Separation or divorce is indicated if the line divides in half (see Figure 78).

A number of lines suggests several serious relationships during the person's life and also reflects a warm and giving nature; the absence of lines indicates the opposite. For instance, I recently examined a man's hand that didn't show even the faintest trace of a line—yet he's been married to the same woman for 30 years and they have three children. Without even meeting this man's wife, I pitied her, since the absence of a Marriage line confirmed the other things I found in his hand, which revealed many self-gratifying, egotistical features. Although his sensuality was evidenced by his distinctive Mounts of Venus and Luna, the soft and flabby texture of his skin—along with the puffy third phalanges of his fingers—suggested a tendency toward excess in food, drink, or sex, and a lack of physical fitness.

Figure 78

Vertical Markings

Vertical lines on the Mount of Mercury (see Figure 79) are an indication of a nurturing personality, which includes the care of animals. Since these lines do tend to depict an interest in children, they often appear in the hands of parents, but they're just as likely to be encountered on the hands of nurses or veterinarians (whether they're parents or not).

The Bracelets

The wrist section generally shows three distinctly marked rings, called "The Bracelets." They have little importance in the evaluation of the hand except to confirm the individual's overall state of health.

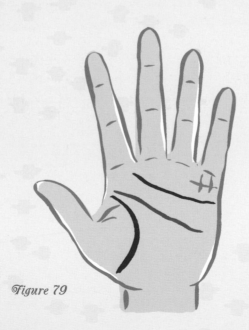

Figure 79

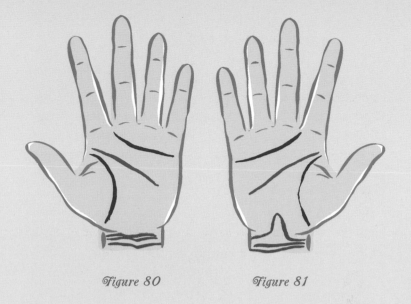

Figure 80   *Figure 81*

- If the Bracelets are distinct, clearly defined, and lie parallel to each other, this points to a robust and healthy constitution (see Figure 80).

- Should the first Bracelet closest to the wrist (see Figure 81) rise upward into the palm, this is said to be a sign of a malfunction in the reproductive organs, whether or not the subject is a woman or a man.

  It's believed that in Ancient Greece, before a woman could get married, she had to appear before a priest to have her hands examined. If the first Bracelet rose up into her hand, this was seen as a sign of infertility. The priest wouldn't give permission for the marriage, and the young woman was subsequently made a vestal virgin of the temple.

Having explained the various characteristics of the lines and markings on the hands, I'd like to share with you how I can use the lines on an individual's hand as a time guide. After all, the most common questions that people ask me are: "Can you tell me when I'm going to get married?" or "Will I have a long life?" and so forth. Even though I refrain from making such predictions, there is an *approximate* time frame that can be estimated from the lines. The next chapter will explain how I do so.

The Palm As a Time Guide

*A*n approximate time frame for an individual's life can be obtained from analyzing the Life, Head, and Fate lines, *but I implore my readers to keep in mind that these are hypothetical measurements and therefore not to be taken factually.*

The Quick Time Guide

An easy way to estimate a person's time frame is to draw an imaginary line from the tip of their Saturn finger toward their Life line (see Figure 82, page 138): The

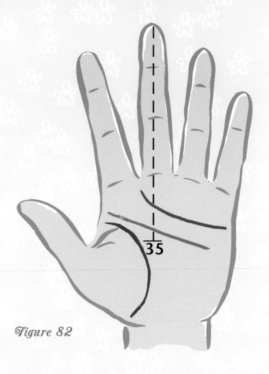

35

Figure 82

point of intersection marks approximately 35 years of age. While this point reflects the middle of the Life line's course for many hands, it does vary from hand to hand due to the difference in the size and especially the shapes of palms. According to Judith Hipskind's book *Palmistry: The Whole View*, if both sections of the Life line before and after this imaginary meeting point are approximately equal in length, the years represented on each side share equal significance; if the length before the point of intersection is shorter than the length after it, a person's remaining years will carry greater weight than the years before the point did.

The System of Seven

Cheiro and other palmists used "The System of Seven" as a yardstick for measuring time. The number seven is highly important in occult sciences and in ancient religious practices, including the Kabbalah (and even the "seven days of the week"). In more recent times, Gail Sheehy applied the span of seven years to identify the stages people go through during their lifetime in her book *Passages.*

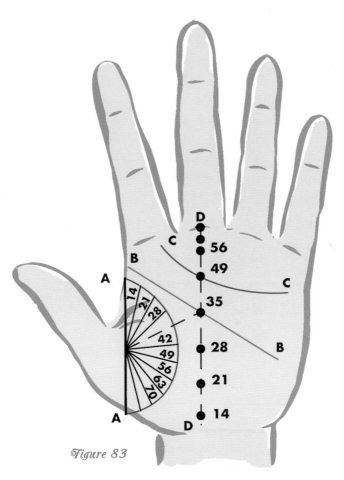

Figure 83

Time on the Life Line

The Life line is divided into increments of seven years, starting from its beginning point above the thumb (see Figure 83, line *A*, page 139). It's of utmost importance to compare the Life lines in both hands. I personally believe that lines can and do change with time, for they register our development—this is especially prevalent in an individual's dominant hand.

If you happen to have a short Life line that doesn't complete the circle around the Mount of Venus, don't despair, for this isn't an indication that you're going to die young. If you have a short Life line in the left (birth) hand and one of average length in the right (dominant) hand, it may simply mean that you had a congenital predisposition toward an illness that never materialized. Whatever the case may be, one can inherit *tendencies* toward a disease, not necessarily the disease itself. However, if the length of your Life line is of great concern to you, this should give you an incentive to lead a healthy life by eating and exercising properly.

Time on the Fate Line

- If the Fate line starts from or near the wrist, such an individual probably feels a strong sense of purpose or commitment at an early age (see Figure 83, line *D*, page 139).

- If the Fate line stops when intersecting with the Head line (see Figure 83, line *B,* page 139), which marks an approximate age of 35 years, this signifies that the person isn't contemplating new challenges at this point. This individual is either very satisfied with their life and achievements and isn't reaching for new goals, or it may reflect stagnation.

- If the Fate line extends past the Head line and intersects with the Heart line (see Figure 83, line *C,* page 139), this would indicate an approximate age of 50 and could provide an important clue that a change is approaching for the individual, most likely in their personal life.

- A Fate line forging beyond the intersection of the Fate and Heart lines reflects ongoing efforts to embrace new challenges and adapt to life's situations. This also points to a strong life philosophy, especially if the Fate line reaches its destination of the Mount of Saturn.

- A Sister line (see page 123) that accompanies the Fate line for a while shows support of the main line and reinforces the above statements.

CHAPTER 11

Analyzing Both Hands Together

*I*t's extremely important to examine both hands of a person—for although they may look alike on the surface, the trained eye of a palmist will zero in on major, as well as slight, differences between them. If a person is ambidextrous, this should be taken into consideration as well.

It's also quite interesting to look at a newborn baby's hands and follow their development periodically in order to observe how and when hands begin to change.

How the Brain Works

The human brain is the most finely tuned computer in the world. I assume that most people are familiar with its division into the nonverbal *right* side and the verbal *left* side. The right half of the brain is developed in the fetus and is associated with perceptions rather than analysis; the left side reveals how we process the information we receive from the right side of the brain and also dictates most of the functions of the right side of the body, including the right hand. It shouldn't come as a surprise that the right hand tends to becomes the dominant one, although both hands receive messages and commands from the brain through the central nervous system, just as the two halves of the brain correspond with each other through the dense bundle of nerve fibers called the *corpus callosum.* But, even though some people have worked hard to develop one side of their brain or the other, right-handed people are generally "left-brained," which means that they tend to depend mostly on logic and analysis; left-handed people are predisposed to be "right-brained," or more artistic, relying fundamentally on first perceptions and "hunches."

My Own Hands

To illustrate the differences and changes that can occur in the hands, I'm going to use my own as an example, since I can readily verify or disclaim the data observed. I'm also of a mature age, chronologically speaking, so my central nervous system has had many years in which to register changes.

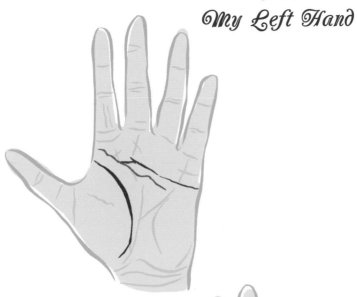

Figure 84
My Left Hand

Figure 85
My Right Hand

Unchanged Characteristics

These include the basic shapes of my hands and fingers, which are a combination of the Philosophic/Intellectual and the Social/Artistic hand types. The primary type (Philosophic/Intellectual) is indicated by my long fingers and distinctive finger and thumb joints; the influence of the Social/Artistic hand type is shown in the longer shape of my palm, my rounded fingertips and well-developed Apollo fingers, and the Apollo lines in my right hand (see Figure 84—My Left Hand; and Figure 85—My Right Hand, page 145).

- The Life line follows a similar course in both hands, with the starting and ending points approximately in the same place. The Life lines on both of my hands possess Influence lines that accompany them, reflecting resistance toward illness and infections. I can readily confirm this—I've indeed been blessed with excellent health and energy.

- Both hands have a Mars line, which is seen on the inside of the Life line descending from the Mount of Mars. Such a line is indicative of a person's fighting spirit and perseverance, which can be used positively toward competitive endeavors and endurance, or negatively in the form of destructive and aggressive behavior. I would like to think that, for the most part, I've made use of this energy by channeling it into productive and creative endeavors.

- Although it's difficult to assess from a handprint, both of my thumbs have firm base joints, showing a measure of self-control and stability. But my first, or nail joints, indicate greater flexibility, which reflects a readiness toward accepting new challenges.

Changed Characteristics

The most drastic change between my hands occurred in the course and positioning of the Head and Heart lines, which in any pair of hands is significant, as it involves two major lines. As you'll observe from Figures 84 and 85, the Head line in both of my hands is widely separated from the Life line, which reveals an inborn spirit of independence—but on the negative side, this is a sign of impulsiveness and rashness in making decisions, a characteristic I unfortunately do possess.

- A considerable change is seen in the Head line, which is shorter on my left hand. Here, it ends under the Mount of Apollo, which is considered to be average in length, but its quality is weakened due to its waviness, for this generally reveals an irresolute nature.

   Branches or forks from the Head line are present in both hands, but they start from different points. On my left hand, I have the Writer's Fork, which starts beneath my Saturn finger and continues toward the Mount of Luna. I have always enjoyed writing, and have kept a diary and a vast private correspondence for most of my life.

In my right hand, the Head line is considerably longer, ending under the Mount of Mercury. Fortunately, it also follows a somewhat straighter course than in my left hand. Here, the Writer's Fork descends from the Head line later on, between and beneath the fingers of Saturn and Apollo, which would suggest an avocation for writing around the age of 40—indeed, this is when I began to write about graphology.

- Probably the greatest difference between my hands lies in the positioning of the Heart and Head lines. As you can see, the Heart line on my left hand starts below the finger of Saturn, forming a partial Simian line, with an Influence line connecting the Head and Heart lines. The point where this "near fusion" takes place suggests approximately 25 years of age. In fact, I did at this point commit an act of folly concerning my affections, making a very important decision based on feelings and hunches without even the most superficial investigation. I turned a deaf ear to the advice of family and friends. Such boldness and rashness is also confirmed in the wide separation of the Head and Life lines at their beginning point, while a lack of objectivity is revealed in the narrow space between the Head and Heart lines (the Quadrangle).

- The existence of at least a partial Girdle of Venus (see Figure 75, page 129) in my left hand exhibits a desire for adventure and excitement . . . as well as mood swings and susceptibility to outer stimuli. This line is absent in my right hand (except for a few fragmented markings), so this decreases some of the characteristics of the Girdle of Venus.

- As mentioned previously, both of my thumbs are firmly rooted and are of more-than-average length. What can't be seen from the handprints is that my left thumb is set more firmly at the top section than my right one is, suggesting greater flexibility and versatility in the latter. Since my right hand displays a more advantageous positioning and formation of the principal lines of Head and Heart—seen in the wider Quadrangle—the possession of a more flexible thumb in the dominant hand can be viewed quite favorably.

- Both of my hands have a Fate line that runs from the inside of the Life line near the wrist. This reveals a strong influence or interference from family during my early years. Yet the course and length of the Fate line is quite different on each hand.

    In my left hand, the Fate line stops before reaching the Head line, around my 25th year. This coincides with what I described above regarding my Heart line. This also indicates that my career goals were interrupted at that time.

    The Fate line in my right hand continues toward the Mount of Saturn, its destination point. The presence of a Sister line, which accompanies the main line, and a second Fate line, which ascends from the Heart line upward, suggests ongoing efforts and a desire for new challenges or personal growth.

• My left hand is devoid of any Apollo lines, but my right palm displays two lines starting from the Heart line and ascending toward the Mount of Apollo. This would indicate that my creative abilities were developed later in life, which is confirmed by the presence of the Writer's Fork.

The rounded outer edge of my right hand, below the Mount of Mercury (the Percussion), further emphasizes the use of my creative energy. This reveals resourcefulness and ingenuity, a feature that isn't present in my left hand.

ℒeaning 𝒯ingers

When holding up both of my hands, as if to make a gesture, the fingers in my left hand are well separated, which reveals a spirit of adventure. However, the Apollo finger in my right hand leans toward Saturn, which suggests an excessive need for material or emotional security. After discovering this undesirable characteristic from my own hands, I'm now consciously trying to keep these two fingers apart, since an excessive need for security is a hindrance to my personal growth.

The Jupiter Finger

My left index finger is shorter than my right one, which suggests greater assertiveness in career situations than in private matters. I consider this to be correct.

Conclusions

Having completed the comparison of my hands, I admit that I'm pleased with having developed my creative and intellectual abilities. Looking back at my early life, especially to my teens and early 20s, some of the tendencies that were indicated in my left hand could have proven perilous. The more favorable features in my right hand may have been the result of a strict but stable upbringing and social environment during my childhood and adolescence. Furthermore, I also believe that some of the positive characteristics revealed in my hands, such as firm and long thumbs, as well as my "knuckles of philosophy" (the distinctive top joints in my fingers and thumbs)—a feature I used to detest—have helped me gain insight and self-knowledge. This allows me to admit the weak spots I need to work on and encourages me to persevere in tough situations.

CHAPTER 12

Fingerprints and Patterns

*T*he corrugated texture of the skin on the palm and fingertips has two purposes: (1) It promotes the stimulation of the nerve endings beneath the top layers of the skin; and (2) it contains secretion channels for perspiration. In some people, the ridges of the skin on their hands are extremely fine, while others' skin patterns can be read with the naked eye. I advise that you always have a magnifying glass on hand so that you don't miss important details when examining the palmar surface.

The Classification of Patterns

Fingertip patterns can be classified into four basic designs:

1. The Loop
2. The Whorl
3. The Low or Simple Arch
4. The Tented Arch

Among these primary types of patterns are infinite subgroupings and variations. The number of capillary ridges surrounding the patterns vary, and no two are alike—from person to person, or even from finger to finger. Therefore, fingerprints make excellent unique, individual calling cards.

1. The Loop

This pattern has three noteworthy variations: *Ulnar; Radial;* and *Composite,* which is a combination of the Ulnar and Radial loop formations.

- The **Ulnar loop** is the most frequently encountered pattern on human hands. As you can see in Figure 86, the pattern leads in from the outer edge of the finger, with the ridges exiting out from the side they enter. The loop formation also usually has one triangle.
  The characteristics associated with this pattern are versatility and adaptability in the

face of life changes—people who possess many Ulnar loops aren't confined to narrow viewpoints. But if such loops are encountered on all ten digits, which is rather rare, there may be a tendency toward a lack of firmness and/or stability in the personality. This would have to be confirmed by other findings in the hand, such as extremely flexible fingertips, a presence of the Girdle of Venus, and other loops found on all fingers. A firm, strong thumb would provide an excellent balance to this pattern.

- The **Radial loop** pattern (see Figure 87) enters the fingertips from the opposite direction as the Ulnar loop—that is, from the thumb side of the palm. The Radial loop also possesses one triangle.

   This loop formation is found relatively infrequently. When it *is* present, it's most often encountered on the thumb or index fingers. People who possess the Radial loop tend to be extroverted by nature and like to impress others, which might be construed as

Figure 86   Figure 87

bragging. Individuals with this pattern also tend to seek new stimuli and challenges. According to *The Book of the Hand,* by Fred Gettings, the characteristics associated with the Radial loop are similar to those of the Whorl pattern (see next page), and having such loops is an indication of originality and individuality.

- Another variation of the loop pattern is the **Composite loop**, which is essentially a combination of the Ulnar and Radial patterns (see Figure 88). Resembling the letter *S,* the Composite loop has two distinct sets of curves and two triangles.

  People who possess Composite loops can see both sides of everything. In problem-solving, they may see several solutions, but when it comes to making decisions, these individuals tend to find it difficult to make up their minds. Thus, due to their lack of decisiveness, they may miss opportunities. It's important to observe in which finger or thumb this pattern appears—if found in the right hand, it's more significant.

2. The Whorl

The Whorl is an easily recognized pattern: It's shaped like a wheel, with a tiny knot or "peacock's eye" in the middle, and surrounding lines winding concentrically around it. The Whorl generally has two triangles supporting the core on either side (see Figure 89). The Whorl in Figure 90 is in actuality a combination of two or more types of patterns, yet since it possesses two triangles, it would be classified as a Whorl pattern.

According to ancient Chinese philosophy, yin and yang are the opposite, primordial forces that make all phenomena possible. *Yin* is the centrifugal force and is associated with all things feminine and passive; *yang* is the contractive force and is representative of the masculine, active forces. Chinese palmists also applied the yin and yang theory to the patterns on fingerprints, claiming that whoever possesses the Whorl pattern is endowed with an independent spirit and originality. People with this pattern on their fingertips are said to not only have brilliant minds, but they're also believed to be highly strung and impatient. As a result, such individuals may suffer from stomach ailments.

The Whorl is the most complicated of all of the patterns, and it belongs to the most complex personality type, psychologically speaking. If encountered on hands with many positive characteristics, the favorable qualities are enhanced, but in hands that reveal many negative traits—such as weak thumbs or unfavorable major lines, the presence of a Simian line and Girdle of Venus, the absence of a Fate or Apollo lines, or an exaggerated development of the Mounts of Venus and Lower Mars—the negative findings would dominate. Furthermore, too many Whorls in one hand is considered excessive. The wisdom of the ancient Chinese palmists proclaimed that if there were more than five Whorls present in the two hands, the favorable characteristics associated with this pattern would be erased.

3. The Low or Simple Arch

This pattern resembles a raised bridge, and lacks angles, triangles, or upthrusts (see Figure 91). An example of this can be found on the palm of the orangutan from Chapter 4 (Figure 15, page 48). As you can see from the illustration, the orangutan shows clearly marked Simple arches on three of its fingers, while the pattern on the index finger suggests an Ulnar loop formation.

The Arch pattern occurs in less than 10 percent of all human hands, and when it does makes its appearance, it's usually encountered on the Jupiter finger among the Elementary/Primitive hand types.

People who possess the **Low arch** pattern are security minded for themselves, their families, and their communities. They take their commitments very seriously; at the same time, they may be resentful of these self-imposed burdens.

Figure 91

One of the less admirable characteristics ascribed to the Simple arch pattern is stubborn defiance and a lack of insight into themselves and others. Since these individuals often find it difficult to express their feelings, their tempers have a tendency to erupt like volcanoes. These people should be encouraged to engage in some form of physical activity, which would allow them to discharge feelings of hostility in a nonaggressive way.

4. The Tented Arch

This is the least common of all of the patterns. **The Tented arch** gets its name from the upright central core that resembles a tent pole, with the capillary ridges draped around it (see Figure 92). The Tented arch has a triangle and an upthrust, and is most likely encountered on the Jupiter finger.

As with the Loop formation, people who possess the Tented arch have quick mental and emotional responses. Yet, like those with the Whorl formation, these individuals are also high-strung by nature, and they thrive on action. This pattern is also associated with individuality and an inborn appreciation of the arts in diverse areas.

One of the by-products of this pattern is the high degree of idealism that these people always have. This may not always prove to be a favorable characteristic, though, since it doesn't reflect a down-to-earth approach in certain situations. So when it comes to solving problems, their idealism and practical consideration could be at odds with each other. A square-shaped palm, which shows practicality, and a firm thumb of at least average length would provide a good balance for this inborn pie-in-the-sky idealism.

Figure 92

CHAPTER 13

How to Take Handprints

*I*t's important, as well as interesting, to record the findings that are obtained from the hands you examine for future reference and for research purposes. Once you've taken a handprint, it's most helpful to preserve the results on a data sheet. Following are the easiest ways I know of to take handprints.

The Outline of the Hand

The best way to take an outline of a hand is to place it on a sheet of paper, palm side down, and carefully trace around the fingers, thumb, and the contour of the hand. It's often easier to do one's own outline rather than have someone else do it.

After you have an outline of both hands, draw in the major lines of Life, Head, and Heart. Accuracy is of utmost importance, since the positions of these lines are the focal point of the entire palm. Next, draw in the minor lines, being as precise as possible regarding their distance, positions, and starting and ending points. Continue by drawing in the respective finger and thumb sections, being specific about their relative length. Note the color and shapes of the fingernails, as well as the patterns on fingers and thumb tips. This information can be recorded directly above each finger and thumb.

As I mentioned in the last chapter, I always keep a magnifying glass on hand so I can examine each finger-tip pattern. I make a note of the respective Loop, Whorl, Simple or Tented Arch I see, and later copy this information on to the data sheet.

Printing with Ink

This method of obtaining prints is and has been widely used with apparent success. Personally, I haven't had the best results because of smearing, which distorts the patterns. In addition, when copying a thin hand, I find that the center of the palm doesn't get printed, in spite of pressing the hand down firmly on the paper. However, my lack of accomplishment shouldn't deter others from trying this method.

Below are the products (which can be found in most art-supply stores) to make handprints in ink:

- A tube of water-soluble printer's ink

- A 5" rubber roller

- A piece of glass or plexiglass, 8" by 10" or larger

- A stack of standard-size sheets of paper of fairly good quality, without watermarks

How to Take the Print

Start with a clean, dry palm. Squeeze the printer's ink onto the glass or plexiglass, and dilute it with enough water to roll it out so that it coats the rubber roller completely. Coat the palm with the roller, leaving no spaces blank. Then press the hand down firmly on to the paper without shifting it. Remove the ink by wiping it off with paper towels, followed by the application of a lanolin-based hand-cleaning product.

Printing on Smoked Paper

In the "old days," before the age of copying machines, palmists often used this method for obtaining handprints. It was a simple, inexpensive method, and the products needed were readily available. It's still a useful method today.

How to Take the Print

"Smoke" both sides of a sheet of good-quality paper, without watermarks, over a candle (obviously, pay attention that you don't burn the paper). Press the hand down firmly and evenly on the paper's surface. After the hand-prints are done, an acrylic fixative (or even hair spray) should be applied to the paper in order to preserve the prints and keep them from smearing. The handprints should be stored with tissue or waxed paper between them so that they don't smudge.

The Copying Method

My favorite method of recording handprints is to use a good copying machine. An additional advantage of this method is that it's available to just about anybody.

How to Take the Print

The hand should be placed, palm side down, on the surface of the copying machine, just as if you were copy-ing a page of paper. If you're doing this by yourself, you can only do one hand at a time, but if someone else is there to assist you, both palms can be placed side-by-side on the machine (use legal-sized paper). Don't forget to replace the cover of the copying machine over the hands before printing. It's also a good idea to place a towel or coat over the lid of the copying machine to avoid over-exposure. Better results are generally obtained by select-ing a lighter rather than darker tone. However, the main criterion is the clear visibility of *all* the lines, especially the major ones.

How to Record the Data

Now that you have an accurate handprint, record your data on a sheet. You should include the following information:

1. **Personal information.** List the subject's name, sex, age, if they're right- or left-handed (or ambidextrous), and the date of the evaluation.

2. **Hand type.** Record if the hand is Elementary, Square, Spatulate, Conic, Philosophic, Psychic, or Mixed, or if it's a combination of types.

3. **Thickness of the hand and palm.** Write if the hand is thin/soft, thin/hard, firm/elastic, thick/hard, thick/firm, or thick/soft. Make a note if the center of the palm is hollow.

4. **Color of palm and lines.** Are they white, pink, or red?

5. **Depth of the Life, Head, and Heart lines.** Indicate if they're deep, broad, clearly marked, or thin.

6. **Skin texture.** Record if it's fine, medium, or coarse.

7. **Length of fingers compared to the palm.** Are they long, average, or short?

8. **Shapes of fingers.** Are they square, spatulate, thick, thin, or tapered? Note anything unusual, such as malformations.

9. **Finger sections.** Observe if one of the three sections dominates.

10. **The size of the thumb.** Is it short, average, or long? Notice whether the first or second section dominates or if it's balanced.

11. **Shape of the thumb.** Note if it's square, thick, or thin, and if the second section is tapered or thick.

12. **Thumb setting.** Is it high, low, or in between?

13. **Patterns of fingerprints of all ten digits.** Write down all of the Loops, Whorls, Simple Arches, or Tented Arches that you see.

14. **Fingernails.** Indicate if they're long/broad, short/broad, short/small, conic/rounded, conic/tapered, talon-shaped, or dish-shaped.

15. **Texture of fingernails.** Note if the nails are smooth, or if they have vertical or horizontal ridges or white spots.

16. **Color of fingernails:** Are they white, pink, blue/gray, or red? Also check to see if any semicircular moons are present.

17. **Development of the Mounts:** Note which mounts—Jupiter, Saturn, Apollo, Mercury, Venus, Luna, Lower Mars, or Upper Mars—are distinctive or flat.

Now that you've been introduced to the physical aspects of the hand, and you've seen how the myriad of lines and markings on an individual's palmar surface can point to their intellectual and emotional development, you're ready for the practical applications of palmistry.

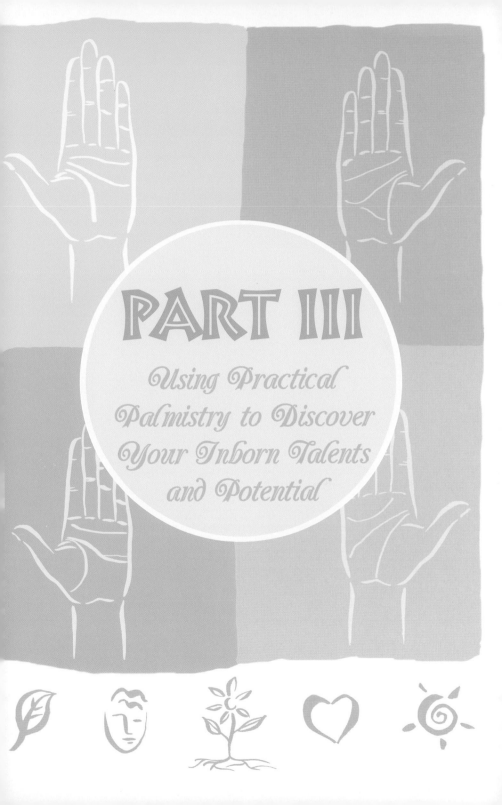

PART III

*Using Practical
Palmistry to Discover
Your Inborn Talents
and Potential*

CHAPTER 14

Gestures:
The Language
of the Hand

*H*ands play a very important role in nonverbal communication. Gestures are as much governed by the brain as spoken or written words are. Since most people are unaware of what they reveal with the movements of their hands, they usually don't manipulate them to mask their feelings, as one might do with a "fake smile" or insincere words. For this reason, hand gestures tend to be more sincere than what people express with their eyes or mouths.

Our hands—through their liveliness or stiffness, and by the positioning of the individual fingers and thumbs—disclose what we most strongly feel in social situations. Hand gestures generally mirror the context of verbal communication and can express a wide range of emotions. They can reflect anything from our uneasiness, frustration, and fear to our joy and spirit for adventure and new experience.

As you might guess, gregarious or extroverted people use their hands more freely to illustrate a point, but keep in mind that erratic or jerky hand movements tend to reflect a state of agitation or nervousness.

A fun experiment is to try watching a TV show with the volume muted—chances are, you'll be able to follow the plot almost as well as if you had the sound on. All you have to do is concentrate on the actors' gestures. Watching the hands of public figures when they appear on TV is also an excellent way to observe them and get a feel for what they stand for.

I would like to share some gestures with you to illustrate the "language of the hands."

Figure 93

A gesture of enthusiasm and spontaneity is displayed in Figure 93 by the widely spaced fingers and thumbs on this woman's left hand. The way her very flexible fingers bend backward, and the angle of her arched thumbs, reveals that she would be extremely receptive to outer stimuli. Her arched thumbs also reveal a tendency toward spending money, time, and affections liberally.

Figure 94

An air of confidence is shown in this man's right hand. While his fingers are held firmly together, disclosing a measure of reserve and caution, his outstretched thumb reveals an aggressive nature.

Figure 95

Here, a congresswoman is speaking with confidence and assertiveness, yet these characteristics are tempered by an attitude of caution, which the close spacing of the Saturn and Apollo fingers on her right hand reveals. The fingers on her left hand are broadly spaced, which shows her adherence to traditional values, and the Jupiter and Mercury fingers are separated widely, expressing her independence of thought and action.

Figure 96

Clasped hands is a sign of uncertainty, especially if the thumbs are hidden inside the fist. Conversely, a clenched fist is usually a sign of determination, revealing a measure of anger or aggression. Figure 96 illustrates this on the left hand of a female lawyer. Her long thumb, stretched out at a maximum angle, points to her resolve and assertiveness.

Figure 97

Another gesture of an assertive nature is the pointing index finger. This is a statement of authority, whether made by a parent, teacher, or politician stressing a point.

Figure 98

The index finger pointed into the air, illustrated in Figure 98 by an athlete, is a gesture of enthusiasm. It also reveals a competitive spirit.

Figure 99

Explaining or debating an issue in a positive, confident manner is demonstrated by the well-separated fingers in Figure 99. The strong and somewhat stiff thumbs are a sign of independence—but they also indicate a measure of stubbornness.

Figure 100

The confident attitude is absent in the hands of this politician. His partially closed hands and bent fingers belie his smile. These hands reveal his uneasiness with the topic being discussed or presented.

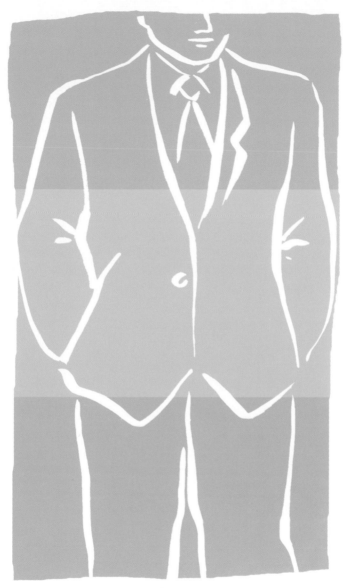

Figure 101

Hands in pockets is a gesture that shows caution. It tends to reflect a "wait-and-see" attitude, and is often a sign of self-consciousness.

Figure 102

Hands folded behind a person's back indicate that they may be holding back some information that they don't want to expose. Figure 102 shows a politician speaking to the public with his hands hidden behind him . . . he's assuredly not revealing all of his cards!

Figure 103

Hands folded loosely in front of a person display an attitude of conservative confidence. Such a gesture would belong to someone comfortable with leadership, but who is also receptive to the opinions of others.

183

Figure 104

Figure 105

Hands or fingers covering the mouth or face are never a sign of confidence. The dispositions may range from discomfort and indecisiveness to dishonesty. For example, the person in Figure 104 appears to be uncomfortable or uneasy, whereas the tightly locked fingers in front of the man's mouth in Figure 105 reveal a measure of deviousness.

Figure 106

Covering the mouth and face with the palm outward, as if to push things away, reveals not only a defensive and defiant attitude, but it's also a gesture that expresses fear or discomfort.

Figure 107

Arms folded in front of the chest signifies authority, but it may also be a gesture of defiance or belligerence. The person may not be revealing all that they know, especially if their arms are folded so that you can't see their hands at all.

Figure 108

Hands on hips is a gesture made by someone who is in an authoritative position. Figure 108 shows a young woman talking down to a dog at her feet (not shown). Such a stance may also be observed in parents or teachers talking to children.

Figure 109

Hands folded and covering the face or the top of the head is a gesture of despair or uncertainty, especially if the head is lowered to the chest, as shown in Figure 109.

Figure 110

A gesture of prayer is displayed in Figure 110. With her palms extended upward, this woman appears to be asking someone in a high position for help. Upturned palms is most often the signal made by people who are soliciting aid, and it's frequently made by politicians and public figures asking for support.

Positions of Fingers

Along with hand gestures, the positioning of the individual fingers expresses a person's most prevalent social attitudes. These are a combination of developed and acquired social skills, as well as inborn tendencies. Therefore, by the time a person reaches adulthood, the position of the fingers and thumbs is unlikely to change drastically, except if they've experienced shock or illness or are faced with a serious problem.

The positioning of the fingers and thumbs can be ascertained by asking someone to place both hands, palms down, on a tabletop or flat surface in front of them. Have them keep their hands in place while you observe them.

- If the hands are aligned close together on the table, thumbs facing each other, this signifies that the individual is cautious and not a risk taker. It also indicates that they're most likely introverted, not extroverted, people. An extroverted nature is suggested if the hands are widely separated from each other with fingers spaced broadly apart.

- If all fingers are distanced from each other, this reveals spontaneity and a spirit of adventure. If they're *widely* separated from each other, the hand belongs to an expansive or even extravagant personality who hates restrictions of any kind. Taken to extremes, it could be an indication of impulsive and rash behavior.

- When the Jupiter finger reaches toward the thumb, this signifies a desire for independence and new challenges. Conversely, if Jupiter leans toward the Saturn finger, this is a sign of caution and insecurity, which may be rooted in a lack of nurturing during childhood or adolescence. As a compensatory measure, such people often exhibit a need for acquiring material goods, or they may crave approval or affection from others.

- The Saturn finger is the most firmly rooted of all the fingers and for this reason rarely moves toward the other fingers. If Apollo leans toward Saturn, this is a sign of traditional values with a strong need for security. Should the Apollo finger cling to Saturn, this is an unfavorable position, since it suggests that the person is too dependent on emotional or financial security. This would be a hindrance toward personal growth and self-fulfillment.

- If Apollo withdraws too much from Saturn, this shows an extreme attitude on the other side of the spectrum. This individual would reject traditional values, as well as all forms of authority.

- If the Mercury finger is widely separated from Apollo (as if standing by itself), it reflects a powerful desire for independence and an equally fierce dislike of being tied down emotionally. These people may have strong feelings for family and friends, yet they also possess an instinctive fear of relationships that take away their "breathing space." Such a withdrawal of Mercury from Apollo also suggests a difficulty in maintaining close, personal relationships. Since the Mercury finger mirrors our earliest relationships, this attitude may reflect a lack of bonding with parents and siblings. The finger of Apollo is associated with love and relationships, and an extreme separation of these two fingers would indicate a fear of commitment in that area.

- Thumbs that are positioned close to the hand reveal a fear of action and may also be an indication of shyness. Generally, such a person isn't willing to take risks of any kind. Conversely, thumbs bending outward at a wide angle disclose the opposite.

How to Determine the Primary Hand Type

General Information

*I*n the previous chapter, we saw how a person's true disposition could be interpreted from their hand gestures, regardless of what type of hand they have. A person's makeup is born from a mixture of inherent tendencies and acquired trends, which come from our home and social environment and then become an integral part of our personality.

When examining both hands of a person, first consider what they've inherited—that is, the shape and other physical characteristics of the hand itself. Then look at the positioning and spacing of the fingers and thumbs, for this will reveal the person's attitude. Next, look at the lines on the palmar surface for further information regarding the individual's innate abilities, life experiences, and the direction of their energy. Finally, each piece of information should be evaluated as part of the complete picture. To create a thorough profile of a person is not a simple task—it takes time, patience, and insight, and requires a strong desire and interest to elicit the often dormant dreams and talents of the individual before you.

In Chapter 2, I discussed the different hand types, alluding to the fact that there are infinite combinations of hand and finger shapes, lines and patterns, skin texture and color, and so on. Although David Brandon-Jones found it necessary to increase the number of hand types to 12 to illustrate the diversity of hands, Fred Gettings reduced the number of basic combinations to 4, which simplifies the general or preliminary screening of a hand. And by simply taking into consideration the shape and length of the palm relative to the fingers, which is the focal point of any hand, its primary or dominant characteristics become readily apparent.

I've compiled a list of characteristics for each of the four categories—which can work either positively or negatively, depending on whether any trait is exaggerated—and how such qualities fit into the general scheme or composite of the person's evaluation. I'd like to stress once again that it's human nature to possess shortcomings as well as strengths; it's to our advantage to acknowledge them both so that we may build up and capitalize on our power, while being able to work on our weaknesses. This allows us, as human beings, to reach the highest possible level that each one of us is capable of.

The Four Basic Shapes of the Palm

1. Square palm with short fingers — *Practical/Useful personality*

2. Square palm with long fingers — *Intellectual/Analytical personality*

3. Long palm with short fingers — *Dynamic/Social/ Artistic personality*

4. Long palm with long fingers — *Sensitive/Intuitive personality*

I've created personality profiles for each of the four categories, showing inherent tendencies in them all, which I will present for you in the next few chapters. Keep in mind that your hand doesn't need to exhibit *all* of the characteristics listed, but if the majority are present, chances are you fit into that type and will be able to relate to the profile.

In addition, I've included four different handprint samples for each category, in order to demonstrate the diversity within each hand type. This will powerfully illustrate the fact that no two hands are exactly alike.

The Practical/Useful Hand

Characteristics

*P*hysically, the Practical/Useful hand has a square palm with short fingers. The person with this hand tends to:

- seek practical solutions for their problems and ideas;

- be skillful with their hands in one area or another;

- like "hands-on" instruction rather than theoretical "by the book" learning;

- choose physical activity in one form or another;

- be precise, methodical, reliable, and dependable;

- view things in simple "black-or-white" terms;

- acknowledge only what they perceive with logic;

- be steadfast or have a stubborn adherence to opinions;

- respect authority;

- have materialistic values—that is, their practical sense generally outweighs the aesthetic;

- be conservative and adhere to traditional values;

- dislike detail or excessive research, except as it pertains to their particular field; and

- have strong proprietary feelings for family, community, and country.

Profile of the Practical/ Useful Hand

Handprint #1

This handprint (Figure 111) epitomizes the Practical/Useful personality. It belongs to a 58-year-old building foreman in a construction company, a job he seems eminently suited for. This man concentrates on his work with

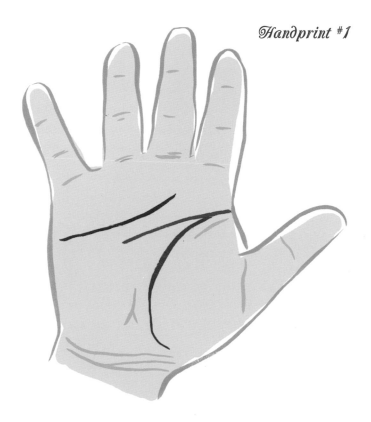

Figure 111

a single-mindedness of purpose, which is indicated by the straight course of his Head and Heart lines. His strong, powerful, and stiff thumb reflects his stubborn adherence to *his* way of thinking—he doesn't possess the mental flexibility to make changes quickly. His long but inflexible Mercury finger shows his practical business sense, and the wide spacing between his Mercury and Apollo fingers is a sign that this man makes decisions independently. However, he may find it difficult to express his feelings easily, so when his anger or frustration reach the boiling point, he'll tend to erupt explosively.

Although people with the Practical/Useful personality often use their hands for physical endeavors, in the pure type you'll actually find relatively few lines engraved upon the square palmar surface (other than the major lines of Life, Head, and Heart). The absence of a Fate line—or any other auxiliary lines, such as Apollo and Mercury—in this hand reveals that this man possesses little insight into himself and others and only understands what he can glean with logic.

Other careers that would fit someone with this type of hand would be agriculture, the military, and all types of "hands-on" work, such as construction and the like.

Handprint #2

This large hand (Figure 112) belongs to a woman about 60 years of age. Although the square palm resembles Handprint #1 with regard to the outline, there are many nuances that set this palm apart. For instance, her Percussion is rather developed, which reflects ingenuity and resourcefulness.

Furthermore, the fingertips in this hand are tapered rather than square, which reveals quick perceptions, adding a third dimension to this personality type. A long, powerful thumb, which is positioned from the palm at an angle of more than 60 degrees, reflects versatility and a daring spirit as well. Her extremely long, tapered Mercury finger points to a talent for communication in music or enterprise—in fact, this woman majored in music and English literature in college.

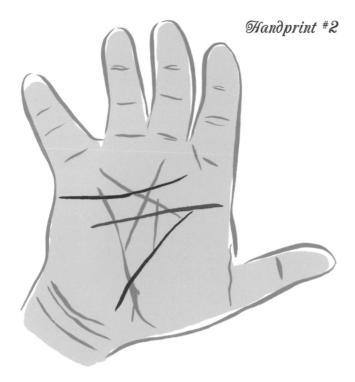

Handprint #2

Figure 112

The straight course of the Head line is inherent for the Practical/Useful hand type, but this lady's Head line is much longer than usual. The average length of this line ends below the Apollo finger, but hers stops beneath the Mount of Mercury, which reveals an exceptional mentality. This is an indication that she would be equally suited for a career in business or law.

The Life line curves in a wide circle around the Mount of Venus toward the Mount of Luna, which confirms a spirit of adventure and love of travel. The presence of two Fate lines shows strong personal or career goals—especially when you take into consideration that when a Fate line appears on this hand type, it's particularly significant.

One of her Fate lines starts from the middle of the palm and surges upward past the Heart line in the direction of Saturn, which expresses ongoing efforts toward achievement and learning. A branch of the Life line (called an "Effort line") is also directed toward the Mount of Saturn, confirming her ongoing projects. The presence of a Mercury line suggests a talent in music or a gift for communication in general, especially since it's coupled with such a long, tapering Mercury finger.

A struggle can also be recognized in this hand: While the thumb and Mercury finger show extroversion and an adventurous spirit that's ready to tackle new challenges, the rest of this person's fingers lean inward toward the Percussion, which reflects an ambiguity or duality in her nature.

Career success would likely occur in these areas: public speaking; politics; business, such as in sales-related areas; or fund raising, where her strong, extroverted qualities and her gift of communication would be an asset. Jobs that place an emphasis on routine work and offer few possibilities for challenges and self-expression would not work out well for this person.

Handprint #3

This hand is considered small compared to the build of the man it belongs to. This is often an indication that such people like to deal with larger issues, tending to leave undesirable details to others.

Handprint #3

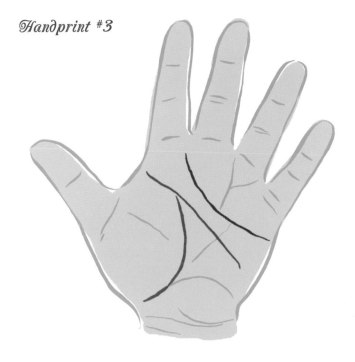

Figure 113

Figure 113 is the left handprint of a 58-year-old engineer. At age 50, this man started his own successful company "from scratch"—as it turns out, many of the characteristics found in his hand indicate that he possesses a knack for business. Evidence for this can be found in his tapering fingers and especially in his rather long Mercury finger, which is called the "Finger of Enterprise." The nail section of this finger is exceptionally long compared to the other phalanges, showing his powers of persuasion. His thick, powerful thumb and longer-than-average Jupiter finger confirm his perseverance, drive, and quest for authority.

This hand, like the previous one in Figure 112, brings opposite forces together. For instance, the rounded Percussion mirrors ingenuity and resourcefulness. The presence of numerous lines—other than just those of Life, Head, and Heart—in this Practical hand further point to the versatility (and ambivalence) in his personality. The Head line is longer than normal and veers toward the Mount of Luna, showing greater imagination and creativity than the pure Practical type would normally possess. In addition, a fork from the Head line, directed toward the wrist, points to an extremely sensitive nature, which highlights the emotional and ambivalent forces within this man's personality. In order to get him to react objectively, one would have to appeal to his intellectual reasoning power.

The presence of a very strong Apollo line, which starts from the Heart line and forms a triangle, reveals that his success would come at the approximate age of 50 . . . which coincides exactly with the opening of his company.

The rather unusual marking of the Poison line here on his dominant hand suggests a tendency toward some form of allergy. As I mentioned earlier (see page 131), this man does indeed have a strong adverse reaction to lobster, as well as to certain medications.

Career possibilities include the fields of: business (in technical/analytical areas), banking, general engineering, and architecture. This man might also find satisfaction in a job as a political leader or career officer, which would combine his brains *and* brawn. But if he had to accept a subordinate position where too much emphasis was placed on details, he would be miserable.

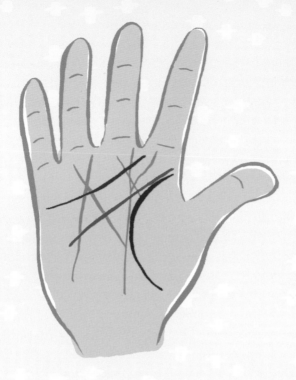

Figure 114

Handprint #4

Since people possessing Practical/Useful hand types are incredibly suited for service-oriented careers such as the military, I'm including the handprint of one of the most famous soldiers of all time: Napoleon Bonaparte. One of Cheiro's most prized possessions was a bronze sculpture of Napoleon's right hand, a photograph of which appeared in his book *Complete Palmistry.* Figure 114 approximates that photograph.

An unusual characteristic for a Practical/Useful hand is a very long, powerful thumb with its tip bent outward at an extreme angle—Napoleon has this, and it shows his enterprising, determined, bold spirit. The fingers all seem to drift toward Jupiter, and since this digit itself is of exceptional length, his quest for power and leadership is evident. In addition, all of his fingers have fully developed nail phalanges, revealing his dynamic physical and emotional energy.

In addition to the major lines, the presence of a Fate line also indicates strong goals and ambitions. A branch from this line travels in the direction of Jupiter at the approximate age of 27, again confirming Napoleon's endeavors toward leadership at that age. His Fate line stops shortly after traversing the Heart line, which represents the hypothetical 50-year mark. Napoleon was 52 when he died in 1821.

It appears that there are two Apollo, or Success, lines present in this remarkable hand, showing the powerful forces of Napoleon's personality. However, a branch of the Fate line crosses with the Apollo line in the Quadrangle, which suggests an approximate time frame of 45 to 50 years of age. This would coincide with Napoleon's downfall at Waterloo when he was 46.

According to Cheiro, one of the negative characteristics in this hand is the positioning of his Fate line. Since it lies too close to the Life line, this points to a personality that's too sensitive and emotional.

Napoleon's hand also falls into the multidimensional category, bringing many opposing elemental forces of the heavy Earth and the dynamic Fire together (see Chapter 20), which may have contributed to his spectacular success, as well as to his great failings.

CHAPTER 17

The Intellectual/Analytical Hand

Characteristics

Physically, the Intellectual/Analytical hand has a square palm with average or long fingers. The person with this hand tends to:

- seek practical solutions to problems and ideas—but uses analytical, theoretical reasoning to arrive at conclusions;

- be able to handle major issues as well as details;

- possess greater versatility than the Practical/Useful type (especially if fingers and thumbs are flexible);

- have a palmar surface that's marked with additional lines beside the major ones, which are reflective of goals, ambitions, and mental flexibility—such as Fate, Apollo, and/or Mercury lines;

- possess managerial qualities, such as being able to see both sides of a problem and "the big picture";

- enjoy a philosophical outlook (if knotty finger joints are present); and

- exhibit great potential for leadership and executive abilities.

Profile of the Intellectual/ Analytical Hand

Handprint #1

This handprint (Figure 115) belongs to a 48-year-old woman who has enjoyed success in many different careers throughout her life. Having once worked as a computer programmer, she's currently setting up the computer system of a small company, where she's also the office manager.

Her square palm indicates that she primarily functions by seeking practical, viable solutions in her life, but her slanting Head line indicates that she's also very creative and imaginative.

Figure 115

In addition to the distinctly marked Life, Head, and Heart lines, many other lines are also etched into this palm. The presence of numerous crisscrossing spiderweb lines (not pictured) reveals an active nervous system and depicts a personality that's far from complacent (perhaps it's even somewhat emotional). The strong thumb and Jupiter finger leaning outward show this woman's receptiveness to new challenges, whereas the relative stiffness of the base section of her thumb and fingers point to self-control and a firm adherence to principles and traditions.

Her distinctive Mount of Venus indicates that she's a very compassionate person, yet she's unlikely to let her emotions interfere with her clear reasoning. The wide spacing between the fingers of Mercury and Apollo shows her independence, and her rounded fingertips reveal her patience and sociable demeanor. Her long Mercury finger also points to good business and communication skills.

Career possibilities include: teaching, caregiving professions (such as nursing or working with animals or children), business, and communications (including public relations).

Handprint #2

Like the woman featured in Handprint #1, this hand belongs to a woman who has an inborn ability to make decisions based on her reasoning power. She also possesses strong managerial and executive capabilities—trained as a laboratory technician, she became a successful sales representative for a pharmaceutical products company. Today, she's the regional manager of a very prestigious company and heads up an entire division by herself.

The fingers in Figure 116 are even longer than those in 115, and they end in tapered, rather than rounded, fingertips. People with such tapering fingertips are usually able to seize opportunities rapidly and instinctively. This woman's very long fingers reflect her patience for details, while her small, square palm shows her ability to grasp the larger issues as well.

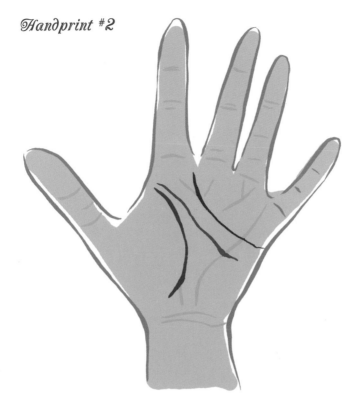

Handprint #2

Figure 116

A rare occurrence for a hand of this type is the extremely long Jupiter finger and thumb leaning outward: This mirrors her readiness for new challenges and her quest for leadership. Her other fingers, though well spaced, stand upright—showing a measure of caution, which is an essential ingredient when embarking on new ventures.

The favorable positions of the major lines on this palm confirm the qualities listed above. The Head line is separated from the Life line at its inception, revealing independence of thought and action, which are inborn tendencies resulting in leadership positions. Her lengthy Mercury finger, with its very long nail phalange, is indicative of a talent for communication and the ability to influence others, which she does with ease and effectiveness. Her elongated, strong thumb lends some necessary staying power and persistence to all of her endeavors.

Suggested careers include: public speaking, publicity, fund-raising, and entrepreneurship.

Handprint #3

This handprint (Figure 117) belongs to a man of 25. The Life, Head, and Heart lines on this palm are positioned extremely well. In addition, other lines are present—namely a distinctive Fate line, which, despite this fellow's young age, already extends past the Head line. This indicates that he has very powerful personal or career aspirations. In addition, his spirit of adventure is clearly shown by his widely separated fingers and long, outstretched thumb. However, his strong common sense is evidenced by the Quadrangle, which is spaced well between the Head and Heart lines.

In this hand, most of the mounts (not pictured) are nicely developed, especially Venus, Luna, and Mercury, as well as Upper and Lower Mars. This suggests that this young man has the desire to lead a full life and that he has the courage to back up his dreams with his actions.

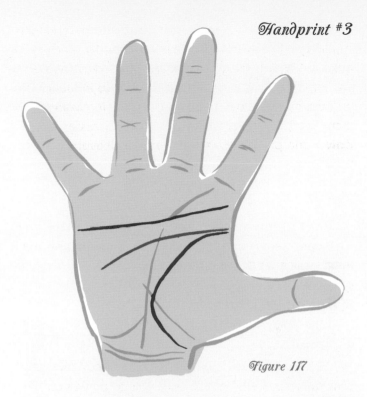

Figure 117

His Apollo finger is considerably longer than his Jupiter finger, which indicates that he isn't a "power-hungry" individual. Instead, he's likely to use his talents in music and communication for the good of humankind. His long Mercury finger reflects his natural proficiency for expression, and his mental faculties are seen in the excellent spacing of the Quadrangle and the long Head line.

After graduating from college early, this young man spent a few years helping underprivileged children in third-world countries. He presently resides in Israel, where he's studying to become a rabbi.

Career possibilities include: public speaking, teaching, medicine, music, or one of the other performing arts. Any job requiring routine, repetitive tasks would be extremely unsatisfying for this type of person, since it would offer them few challenges or opportunities.

Handprint #4

The handprint that this illustration represents (Figure 118) comes from Cheiro's collection, and is shown in his book *Complete Palmistry*. It belongs to Erich von Stroheim (1885–1957), a well-known, successful film director and producer during Hollywood's "Golden Age."

The clarity of the major lines, as well as some of the auxiliary lines, is remarkable. His Head and Life lines are separated by a slight margin at their beginning point, exemplifying independence of thought and action—which is further confirmed by the even spacing of von Stroheim's fingers and thumb. His intellectual and analytical reasoning power is seen in the separation between the Head and Heart lines (the Quadrangle).

The presence of a Fate line starting near the wrist shows early, defined goals. This line is interrupted before it reaches the Head line, which indicates a career change near the age of 30. The long Head line is forked at the end, showing both creative and practical/business abilities; the latter is also exhibited by the ascending fork. The branch slanting toward the Mount of Luna would give a clue to his talent in such creative endeavors as writing. The presence of an Apollo line starting near the wrist and ending at its destination (the Mount of Apollo), further gives a clue to an exceptional personality that was able to survive and conquer adversity.

Handprint #4

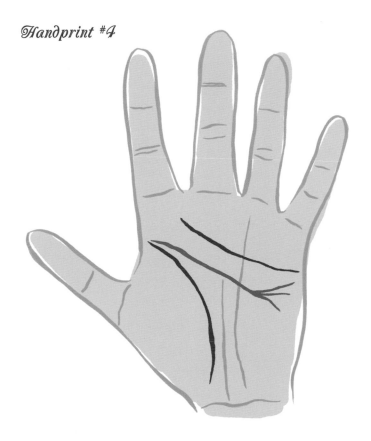

Figure 118

Other career possibilities for someone with this type of hand include: law, banking, entrepreneurship, public speaking, the fine arts, or writing.

The Social/Dynamic Hand

Characteristics

Physically, the Social/Dynamic hand has a long palm with short fingers. The person with this hand tends to:

- possess swift, intuitive perception and a good grasp of ideas;

- act quickly and impulsively and react based on hunches (especially if their fingers are smooth and tapered);

- have good communication skills, either socially or in music or drama—or be a witty conversationalist or storyteller;

- be versatile, but if the fingers are extremely short compared to the palm, this versatility can be taken to extremes—resulting in a flighty personality;

- be intuitive, with an inborn understanding of human nature;

- not be unduly concerned with material or emotional security, so is willing to take risks;

- make generous gestures, especially if somebody appeals to their emotions; and

- be a good salesperson—but they themselves may fall prey to sales tactics used by others.

Profile of the Social/Dynamic Hand

Handprint #1

This handprint (Figure 119) belongs to a woman in her mid-40s who is a coordinator and director of conferences and special events at a small Western college.

Her hand brings together the most favorable features of this hand type—that is, clear major lines of Life, Head, and Heart. Her social skills are seen in the rounded fingertips and distinctive Mounts of Luna and Venus (not shown). The spacing between the Head and Heart lines is wide, indicating that this individual, although emotional by nature, has the ability to make decisions and judgments based on logical deductions. In fact, this type of hand shows a good balance between the emotional and intellectual. The Head and Life lines are joined at the beginning,

Handprint #1

Figure 119

which reveals a conservative personality that's unlikely to do anything in an extreme fashion. The course of the Head line has a gentle curve toward the Mount of Luna, suggesting creative leanings and endeavors. This is confirmed by her long Apollo finger and the presence of an Apollo line starting near the wrist, which reflects inborn creative talent. This lady indeed has a trained, operatic voice, and she continues to sing and perform to this day.

Another favorable characteristic in this hand is her long, strong thumb, which shows staying power and perseverance. The outward angle of her thumb indicates versatility and outer-directed energy, while her straight, evenly spaced fingers suggest a measure of introspection and self-control. Although people with short fingers don't tend to have patience for details, they *will* attend to them selectively in matters that they feel are important. Therefore, these people tend to neglect or avoid matters in areas that don't hold their interest—this woman readily admitted her tendency to procrastinate, and to avoid tasks she dislikes.

Career success would be likely in these fields: acting, personal relations, sales, psychology, or teaching.

Handprint #2

This handprint (Figure 120) belongs to a man in his early 40s who is employed as a staff assistant at the same college as the woman in the previous example. They have a close working relationship, and since their hands are of the same basic type, they seem to have a solid understanding of each other's actions and reactions. Yet these palms also have their differences.

Although this man's palm is oblong, it has a slightly triangular shape that's wider at the wrist in a spatulate formation. Such a person has an absolute need for physical outlets and activities and would not be content in or suited for any job that would chain him to a desk or routine type of work. This man's versatility and adventurous nature is

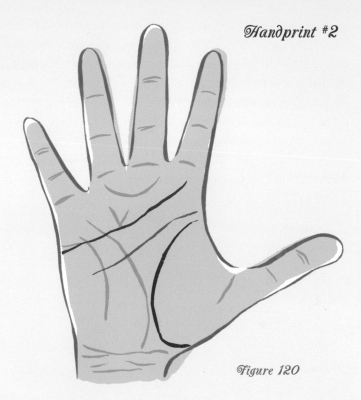

Handprint #2

Figure 120

reflected by his separated fingers, and a thumb that's widely angled away from the palm; and is confirmed by the many additional lines etched into his palmar surface, such as Fate, Apollo, and Mercury lines, as well as a Girdle of Venus and an Intuition Crescent. Indeed, this man is incredibly daring—he enjoys the outdoors, especially mountain climbing—and has many varied interests. For example, he plays several musical instruments, and at the college, he acts as a very stimulating tour guide and conducts many of the social events there. He's also very active in community affairs.

The Fate line starts close to the Life line near the wrist and changes directions a few times. There's also a second or Sister line accompanying it (not shown), which is favorable because it strengthens the main Fate line. The presence of the Girdle of Venus indicates that he is highly attuned to outer stimuli and may be subject to mood swings (which this man admitted was true). The Intuition Crescent at the outer edge of the hand shows that he's highly intuitive, to the point of clairvoyance.

Career possibilities include: acting, politics, fund-raising, sales, and psychology.

Handprint #3

This handprint (Figure 121) belongs to a homemaker in her early 50s, who's married to a very successful physician.

The fingers and thumb in this hand are held closely together, which reveals a rather cautious and conservative nature. From my own observation, this woman *is* somewhat shy and reserved until she gets to know people. The clearness, length, and depth of all of her major lines indicate that she possesses a keen intelligence and the ability for objective reasoning.

The Fate line starting higher up in the palm shows that her goals and the development of her personality were realized later in life, when she was in her 20s. The change of direction in the Fate line points to a major change in her 30s—in fact, this did indeed happen when she left her native India with her husband and two children and came to the United States. Yet the Fate line proceeding past that

Handprint #3

Figure 121

time frame shows that she adapted to her new situation very well. This is confirmed by the smooth skin texture of her palms and fingers, and the flexibility of her fingers and thumb. In addition, the strongly developed Mount of Venus reveals this woman's warmth and empathy, and her love of physical activities, such as tennis. Although of the same type, her hands don't reveal the same versatility or complexity that the previous example showed.

Suggested careers include: teaching, nursing, sales, social work, and tourism.

This handprint depicts Cheiro's own hand, which he included in his book *Language of the Hand.* (Figure 122 recreates the handprint from the book.)

Although Cheiro's hand falls primarily into the Social/Dynamic category, his hand also reflects the influence of the Intellectual/Analytical type—and that of the Psychic/Intuitive, which is evidenced by his long palm. The fingers are tapered, indicating Cheiro's instinctive, intuitive perception and his ability to rapidly grasp ideas. This is also seen in the distinctive Intuition Crescent and in the presence of a cross within the Quadrangle, which is referred to as the "Mystic Cross." All of these features point to a sixth sense and a natural gift of intuition, which Cheiro is said to have possessed in great measure.

Cheiro's intuitiveness allowed him to zero in on the life of the person whose hands he examined. He often made predictions or gave warnings pertaining to future events that he felt could be avoided if the individual exercised caution and good sense. He always had people's best interests at heart, and he lamented the fact that those he tried to forewarn of possible pitfalls, which would result from their own rashness or impudence, often turned a deaf ear to his advice. This is what happened with Oscar Wilde (see page xviii).

Cheiro's hand possesses two Head lines, which is a rather unusual occurrence. One line is meshed closely with the Life line at the beginning point (not shown), revealing a cautious and rather introverted nature, while the upper and more prominent Head line starts high on the Mount of Jupiter, reflecting Cheiro's bold, unconventional ideas and extroverted nature. According to his own

Handprint #4

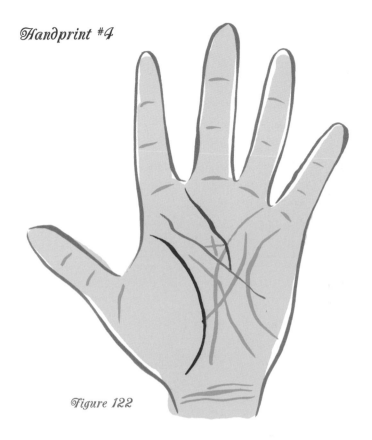

Figure 122

admission, there were two entirely opposite sides to his personality: One was timid, retiring, and loved writing poetry; the other enjoyed the social life and limelight, basking in his lofty professional standing as a highly sought-after palm reader, author, and lecturer.

Cheiro's hand further shows two Apollo lines, one starting low in the palm near the wrist, which is an indication of an inborn artistic talent; the second, more prominent Apollo line intersects with the first one and forms a branch ascending to the Jupiter finger and its mount. This line overshadows even the Fate line, suggesting that Cheiro's ambitions and creative efforts persisted right up to the end of his life.

Other career possibilities for someone with this type of hand include: the fine arts, writing, acting, psychology, law, politics, and teaching.

CHAPTER 19

The Sensitive/Intuitive Hand

Characteristics

Physically, the Sensitive/Intuitive hand has a long palm with long fingers, and generally speaking, the longer the palm, the less practical the person will be. Someone with this type of hand will tend to:

- pay meticulous attention to details;

- be vastly influenced by outer stimuli and circumstances—including music, the visual arts, and nature;

- be moody;

- find it difficult to make quick decisions, for they're trying to adapt their inner needs to outer demands;

- be intuitive and perceptive;

- find themselves affected by the environment—a healthy, peaceful atmosphere is most beneficial for them;

- be contemplative on the surface, but strongly emotional beneath;

- be philosophical and analytical (if the finger joints are well developed);

- have a tendency to be a dreamer (if fingers are smooth and tapered);

- have a talent for dramatic or artistic expression, especially role-playing—which is an excellent attribute for an actor; and

- possess the ability to adapt to people and circumstances.

Handprint #1

The two young women represented here and in the next example are about the same age. When these prints were taken, they were around 18 years old, and both girls contemplated dance as a possible career. It's interesting to compare these two hands.

The handprint pictured in Figure 123 brings out the most favorable characteristics associated with this category. For instance, the alignment and proportions of the

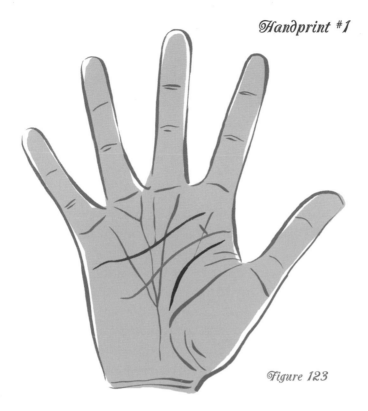

Handprint #1

Figure 123

fingers and the long thumb reveal self-control and enthusiasm. In addition, the Apollo finger leaning toward Jupiter denotes this young woman's potential for leadership, which is confirmed by the Head line starting separately from the Life line. This, coupled with the wide Quadrangle, shows her predilection for objective reasoning. The Head line itself is curving gently toward the Mount of Luna, the center of creative imagination, yet the line has a slight upward turn at the end, indicating a practical sense, which is very beneficial for this hand type.

The presence of an unusually long Fate line for her age suggests that this young lady is endowed with strong goals and principles, as well as a desire for self-actualization. The Fate line's branch toward the Mount of Jupiter shows definite ambition and a strong will, reaffirming her quest for leadership. With the presence of an Apollo line that starts from the Fate line and proceeds on its course toward the Mount of Apollo, I predict that she'll achieve personal and professional success, thanks primarily to her determination and self-control. Her palm has many other propitious characteristics—such as the width of her Quadrangle; the square tip of her Saturn finger; her strong, firm thumb; the excellent balance of her individual fingers; and the major lines that are favorably positioned on her palmar surface—which point to her intelligence and ability to make realistic judgments and decisions.

This young lady has already proven that she can juggle her considerable extracurricular activities with her scholastic achievements. She was the co-valedictorian of her high school and, after having made the decision not to pursue a career in dance, is now attending college. She's planning to major in communications, for which she's eminently suited.

Career possibilities also include: teaching, public relations, law, social work, and psychology.

Handprint #2

The palm in this handprint (Figure 124) is longer and the fingers are shorter than the hand in Figure 123. In fact,

Handprint #2

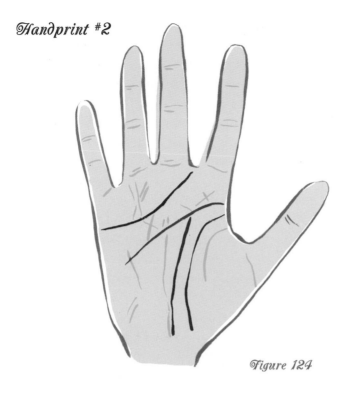

Figure 124

this palm is almost a combination of the Sensitive/Intuitive and Social/Dynamic types, for it blends characteristics from both of them.

This hand shows an unusual configuration with regard to the major lines. The existence of two distinct Life lines reveals a duality in this young woman's personality: She has introverted *and* extroverted tendencies. This dichotomy is also reflected by her Mercury finger, which, although it's of at least average length, is set very low on the palm, suggesting that her need for communication varies—she can be a loner or the life of the party.

The presence of additional lines, such as those of Fate and Apollo, reveal her aspirations, personal goals, and creative endeavors; however, there are numerous horizontal lines crossing the Apollo line, indicating a dispersion of energy. It may also indicate that due to her many interests, she has difficulty making up her mind about what she likes to do best. One clear line of Apollo is more favorable than many, especially if they should cross each other, which is the case with this hand.

The Fate line is tied to the outer Life line, which shows a strong influence from her family; but after its inception, the Fate line proceeds upward into the palm in a straight course, revealing her efforts to achieve and learn. The long Head line and the wide spacing of the Quadrangle on this young lady's palm show her powers of objective reasoning, which is a very significant and favorable characteristic, for it balances her tendency to make impulsive decisions. The wide separation of the Life and Head lines at their beginning points, coupled with smooth fingers, only enhances her rashness.

She possesses a restless nature that craves excitement, and it may be difficult for her at times to resist the temptation of outer stimuli. She needs all of her willpower and emotional maturity in order to say no to substance abuse. This predilection is revealed in the many horizontal markings on the Mount of Luna and the Percussion— these markings may also indicate a tendency toward allergies, but when found in conjunction with the previously mentioned findings, it must be viewed instead as a predisposition toward dependence on drugs or alcohol. Hopefully, her strong thumb and the many other favorable characteristics her hand displays will act as a balance, and help her to resist the lure of activities that are detrimental to her health and future development.

Career success would likely occur in these areas: veterinary medicine or animal care, teaching, and the performing arts (drama, music, or dance).

Handprint #3

This handprint (from Cheiro's collection) is that of four-time British Prime Minister William Gladstone (1809–1898).

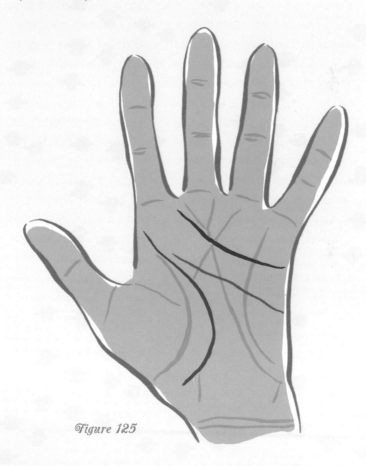

Figure 125

A person with a hand such as this would primarily be an intellectual and a philosopher, as indicated by the long fingers and thumb with pronounced joints. The shape of this palm is oblong rather than square, revealing Gladstone's mental and emotional responsiveness and sensitivity toward the needs of the individual in particular and humankind in general. This is further represented by the multitude of spiderweb lines crisscrossing his palm (not shown), which also reflect the diffusion of energy at this late stage in his life. (The handprint was taken when Gladstone was 88, only a year before his death.) In spite of these delicate lines engraved upon the palmar surface—which points to a fine skin texture—the major lines of Life, Head, and Heart are clearly visible. The exceptionally long Head line starts close to the Life line, revealing a conservative outlook, but then it proceeds independently and curves gently toward the Mount of Luna to the edge of the palm. The length of the Head line, the top sections of the fingers and thumb, and the space marked by the Quadrangle all point to this man's exceptional mental acuity.

The Fate line reflects his exceptional career, for it starts from the wrist near the Mount of Luna and continues in a sweeping course upward into the palm, with strong branches heading toward Jupiter and Apollo. This suggests someone who is comfortable in the limelight, such as a performer or a politician. Although the strong and early inception of the Fate line leaves no doubt that his goals and aspirations at a young age continued on throughout his life, the fact that it starts near the upper part of the Mount of Luna indicates the influence of another person coming into his life at a later date. This could mean a marriage or association with someone in a very visible position.

The existence of an Apollo line starting from the Life line and proceeding uninterrupted to the Mount of Apollo gives a clue to Gladstone's brilliance and to his ability to adjust to life's situations.

In addition to the above lines, the presence of the Intuition Crescent—a line that's inherent to the Sensitive/Intuitive hand type—shows Gladstone's instinctive sixth sense and insight. This must also have been a great asset in his career, for it allowed him to understand others and himself. Judging from his hand and the lines etched into his palmar surface, he must have been a truly remarkable person.

Other career possibilities include: the ministry, medicine, psychology, and law.

Handprint #4

Another example of this category is the hand of famous stage actress Sarah Bernhardt (1844–1923). Cheiro was privileged to take her handprints personally, an event he described in *Cheiro's Complete Palmistry.* (Figure 126 is a drawing based on the handprint in Cheiro's book.) He found Bernhardt's hands to be very remarkable because of the starting and ending positions of the major lines, as well as the clearness and unwavering strength of the Fate and Apollo lines—which reflected her strong personality and the talent that spanned her entire life.

The Life and Head lines on this palm are separated

Handprint #4

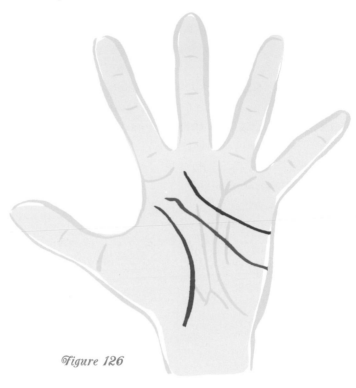

Figure 126

from each other at the beginning point, which reveals independence of thought. Such people often find themselves in leadership roles later in life, whatever their chosen field may be. Bernhardt's widely spaced fingers and thumb display an adventurous spirit and a readiness for new challenges. Her excellent positioning of the major lines, marked by a wide Quadrangle, shows intelligence and objectivity. Such characteristics allow her to make decisions based on clear, practical reasoning, in spite of the hypersensitive nature that's inherent in this type of hand. Her emotional makeup, which responded strongly to outer stimuli, was a contributing factor in her success on the stage.

Bernhardt's hand is further endowed with an Intuition Crescent which, as in the previous example, shows her inborn sixth sense and insight; but unlike that hand, her fingers are smooth and tapered, which reveals quick perceptions and reactions. Her gift of communication is further enhanced and confirmed by her very long Mercury finger. This finger is widely separated from the Apollo finger, which reflects her independence in all areas of her life. This tendency toward aloofness can also be gleaned from the Life line, which curves inward toward the Mount of Venus; conversely, a branch from the Life line headed toward the Mount of Luna reveals a love of travel and/or adventure—here, then, we see the two motivators behind "The Divine Sarah's" personality.

Other career possibilities for someone with this type of hand include: public relations, law, politics, psychology, sales, teaching, writing, design, or architecture.

CHAPTER 20

The Principal Factors of Compatibility

*T*hroughout the ages, matchmakers (professional or otherwise) have tried to find a way to couple people based upon psychological, physical, emotional, and intellectual compatibility. But what exactly, does *compatibility* mean?

While *Webster's* defines it as "capable of existing or operating together in harmony," compatibility between two people tends to refer to their *inborn expectations.* Of course, it's sometimes true that "opposites attract," but people with similar chemistry tend to have a greater rate of success in lasting, long-term relationships than those with diametrically opposed inborn characteristics. Fundamentally mismatched personalities are unlikely to "see eye to eye" with each other. For instance, an individual with a Practical hand type will most certainly expect different things from a spouse or friend than somebody possessing the Social/Dynamic hand. The former values loyalty, responsibility, and steadiness of character, and doesn't mind living with rules and regulations. Conversely, a spouse with the Social/Dynamic hand would find such a regimented life truly boring, as this type tends to desire a diverse life full of activities and challenges.

Therefore, the hand shows several areas where the compatibility between two people can be observed. The major places to look for clues are: the shape of the hand and its proportions, the Heart line, the Mount and Girdle of Venus, and the development of the other mounts.

The Shape of the Hand

The shape of the hand and its anatomical characteristics determine the basic temperament of the individual. Consequently, being able to find the dominant hand type is quite important and should be done carefully and accurately. The most significant factors to pay attention to are the shape of the palm and the length of fingers relative to the palm. As explained previously, a hand may show a combination or influence of several hand types; hand analysis, in fact, consists of evaluating these combinations, but there isn't enough space in this book to show all of them. This infinite range of variations in shapes, proportions, and the linear surface makes a person's hand and personality truly unique. Differences are apparent even in the hands of identical twins—who are born with the same genetic DNA.

Having said this, I'd like to point out that even with all of this diversification, one hand type is usually dominant in each and every human hand—this is its *primary type*. Allow me to summarize what each hand type basically represents.

(Special mention should be given to the Spatulate palm, which is either broader at the wrist section or at the base of the fingers. This type of palm doesn't easily fall into one of the types listed below and should be analyzed by a professional hand-reader.)

1. The Practical/Useful "Earth" Hand

This hand type is characterized by a square palm with short fingers. The palmar surface is marked with few lines beside the Life, Head, and Heart lines. The Head line tends to be straight rather than curving, terminating approximately beneath the finger of Apollo. The skin texture is generally thick or coarse, so the major lines and patterns on fingertips are clearly visible.

People possessing this type of hand are productive, self-reliant, and reliable. They seek practical solutions to problems and usually stick to whatever they decide to take on. Such individuals are the workhorses of the world, and through sheer determination of will, may actually attain greater success than those with quicker minds or a more versatile personality. Far from being dull-witted, the Earth type understands everything that appeals to their logic and solid common sense, but they reject those matters that don't fall neatly into "black-or-white" areas.

The temperament of people with these hands resembles that of the earth itself—solid and heavy. But keep in mind that beneath the earth's crust, there may be a cauldron of volcanic material churning that, when it's ready, can erupt with a terrifying fury.

People with the Earth temperament are devoted to their families or/and communities and feel responsible, protective, and possessive of them, as a mother bear would be of her cubs. The Earth type is able to tolerate routine or repetitive work reasonably well, but generally doesn't care for occupations that require great attention to details. For the most part, physical labor and activities are welcomed by this type.

2. The Intellectual / Analytical "Air" Hand

This belongs to people who are deliberate and pleasant, and who base their decisions upon logical deductions. The hand is characterized by a medium-sized square palm with long fingers and a lengthy, prominent thumb. The skin texture in this type of hand is finer, yet more elastic and flexible, than the aforementioned Earth hand. There are usually additional lines etched into the palmar surface other than the major lines—such as Fate, Apollo, and Mercury lines—although not *all* of them will necessarily be present. The Head line may follow a straight course across the palm or curve gently toward the Mount of Luna, with possible forks in different directions. The fingers of this type are long, and they may be smooth, revealing quickness of thought and perception. Or, they may exhibit pronounced joints, reflecting an analytical, discerning, and philosophical disposition. This type of hand tends to belong to the thinker and intellectual—someone who's a master of logical deduction and reasoning—yet the squareness of the palm confirms that they still have a practical nature. The person with long fingers is able to tolerate working with details or minutiae; therefore, they're ideally suited for research-related careers. If such a hand is also equipped with a long, powerful thumb, it lends perseverance and determination to everything that this person undertakes.

While the Air type is intellectually thorough and deep, they may display a tendency to be emotionally superficial. Such people can easily detach themselves from their private lives while they're attending to their work. Yet, this type is generally known to be fair, with the necessary objectivity that allows them to see all sides of a problem or situation.

People with this type of hand aren't apt to lose their temper, since they can reason things out rationally—unlike the Earth type, who finds it very difficult to express their feelings.

3. The Social/Dynamic "Fire" Hand

This hand is characterized by a long palm and relatively short fingers, which tend to be flexible or tapered rather than stubby or square-shaped. The palmar surface is marked with additional lines beside those of Life, Head, and Heart—the Apollo line is especially prevalent on this hand, signifying creative endeavors and social skills. The skin texture may range from soft and pudgy to firm and elastic (which is the most favorable of all skin textures for any type of hand). The skin itself is generally finer than that of the Earth type; as a result, patterns on the fingertips aren't as easily discerned with the naked eye. The major lines, however, should be clearly defined in order to be considered favorable.

The Fire type of hand tends to belong to people who are socially adept, with a ready charm and a wit to match. They're versatile and perceive things intuitively, so the presence of an Intuition Crescent isn't an unusual occurrence. This type of hand is indicative of a sensitive, emotional person who responds to the moods of the people surrounding them, and to the pulse of the world. The presence of a firmly set thumb of at least average length would lend stability and perseverance to this personality, since the element of fire, when out of control, consumes everything in sight. But when this tendency is held in check, Fire types are dynamic and have a captivating nature.

These individuals tend to thrive on activity and challenges, which is the opposite of Earth people. Routine jobs that demand constant repetition would be unsuitable and boring for them. Short-fingered people aren't known for their patience with people or things; therefore, service-oriented professions, such as social work, nursing, or teaching, wouldn't be their most ideal careers. Instead, they would shine in social situations, or on the stage as actors or politicians. They would also be excellent in sales or public relations, where their gift of communication and inborn charisma would be an asset.

4. The Sensitive/Intuitive "Water" Type

This hand is the most aesthetically pleasing of all of the types. It's characterized by a lengthy, slender palm and elongated, smoothly tapering fingers with long, almond-shaped nails. The skin texture is fine, and in its pure form, the hand feels almost "boneless," which means that it belongs to a person who isn't meant for a harsh life. Of all of the hand types, it's the least suitable for any career that offers practical hands-on experience.

Just like water itself, the Water type is calm and passive on the surface—yet the old adage that "still waters run deep" would justly reflect this personality. Keep in mind that when it's fueled by other forces, such as pitching winds or earthquakes, water can be just as wild and destructive as fire. People in this category tend to be greatly affected by their environment and are highly susceptible to its moods and rhythm. They thrive in a supportive home or social climate, surrounded by beauty in art or music, but they don't have an inborn outer "shell" to protect them from the harshness of life.

This personality type has a tendency to escape into dreaming and role-playing. It shouldn't be surprising that these individuals are eminently suited for careers in the performing arts—such as dance, music, or acting—since impersonating other people or reenacting scenes feels very natural to them. Their smooth, tapering fingers allow for rapid and instinctive perceptions from the world around them, and they're highly attuned to spiritual and psychic vibrations. As a result, they can be excellent mediums and clairvoyants.

As I've said before, hardly anyone's hand is a pure type, and the combination of different categories is often favorable. But as Figure 127 on the following page indicates, some of the elemental types are more or less compatible with each other. For example, Earth and Fire

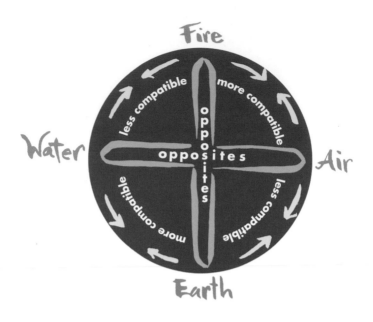

Figure 127

are on the opposite side of the spectrum. The earth is an unmovable, solid mass, characterized by low activity (unless moved by other elements, such as earthquakes); fire is active, versatile, and can consume everything in its path. Consequently, marriage partners with these two opposite types of hands would be emotionally unsuitable. Air and Water are also on the opposite side of the spectrum. The Air type rationalizes everything and leads from their intellect, whereas the Water type, being subjective and emotional, tends to avoid reality altogether and would rather escape into their dream world.

Fortunately, as previously explained, most of us are combinations of two or more hand types, which makes most people well rounded and adaptable.

The Heart Line

This is the second most important factor of compatibility. Its length and direction points to the individual's sexual and emotional nature; the strength and condition of the heart as an organ is indicated by the quality of the line.

Allow me to repeat some of the information I previously presented on the Heart line. (You may want to refer back to Figures 60–64, pages 106–109.)

- A Heart line starting from the Mount of Jupiter, with a gentle curve toward the Percussion, displays a romantic disposition that is loyal and ardent.

- The Heart line starting from the finger of Jupiter itself reveals a high degree of idealism. Such a person would put a loved one on a pedestal . . . which might come crashing down if the object of their affection doesn't live up to their expectations.

- A Heart line starting between the fingers of Jupiter and Saturn shows a deep but calm disposition when it comes to sex. This behavior is between the idealism of Jupiter and the passion of Saturn.

- If the Heart line starts from the Mount of Saturn, this reveals a passionate but self-gratifying nature. This person's own needs are their primary objective. If the Heart line rises from the Saturn finger itself, these unfavorable characteristics are enhanced.

- An excessively long Heart line that lies across the palm from the Mount of Jupiter to the Percussion shows an exaggerated need for love and sexual attention, resulting in a jealous nature.

- A Heart line that's positioned too low in the palm reveals a tendency to let affairs of the heart rule over their common sense and objective reasoning. It also reflects a very sensitive and overly emotional nature.

- A full or partial Simian line (which shows the fusion of the two major lines of Head and Heart), indicates that the individual's emotions and reasoning are permanently interwoven. This is true to a lesser degree in the partial Simian line, or where the two are connected with an Influence line. It's also important to observe in which hand the Simian line appears; if it's found on the dominant hand, or in both hands, it bears a greater significance. People possessing Simian lines aren't easily derailed from their purposes, which they pursue single-mindedly. This can have positive *or* negative ramifications, depending on the intentions of the individual.

It should be evident that people with comparable Heart lines would have a better chance of connecting with each other sexually and emotionally than those with dissimilar lines.

The Mount of Venus

The third major factor symbolizing compatibility in the hand is measured by the Mount of Venus.

A fleshy mount shows a healthy interest in sex and physical activity; it also indicates personal warmth and empathy. An excessively developed mount, however, reveals that these characteristics would be present in extreme proportions. Such a person, by letting basic instincts take over their good sense of reasoning, may be at the mercy of their own sexuality. A flat or underdeveloped Mount of Venus suggests a lack of interest in sexual activity, or it may depict a cold-hearted person who's unable to feel empathy for others.

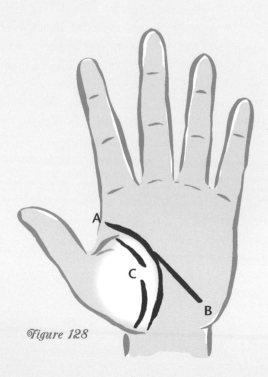

Figure 128

The analyst should also observe the development of the other mounts, which would further clarify where the person's available energy is being channeled. A hand that's void, or shows little development of the mounts, may be compared to an arid wasteland, which could be an indication of a loss of energy resulting from physical or emotional illness. If that's the case, then the skin tone of the person's palm and fingernails would range from gray to blue, depending on the severity of the illness.

The size of the Mount of Venus should also be an important point to observe. The Life line "draws a circle" around it. A wide circle (see Figure 128, line *A*, page 251) reflects a person's desire to lead a full and productive life. This is further enhanced by a branch or branches in other directions, such as toward the Mount of Luna (see Figure 128, line *B*), which indicates a love of travel and adventure. Such a hand tends to be full or fleshy, but it shouldn't be soft or pudgy, for this would reduce the favorable qualities ascribed to it, and would indicate a desire for someone else to provide them with the luxury and comfort they crave.

A narrow or broken Life line encircling the Mount of Venus (see Figure 128, line *C*) would be a most unfavorable configuration, for this reveals a diametrically opposite personality to the one described above, especially if the hand is dry and bony with a hollow-centered palm.

In the Palm of Your Hand

The Girdle of Venus

As I've previously noted, although the Mount and Girdle of Venus (see Figure 75, page 129) bear the same name, they're completely different entities, located in different spheres of the palm. The semicircular Girdle lies in the Emotional zone (at the base of the fingers), while the Mount of Venus is situated in the Physical sphere (at the base of the thumb, inside the Life line).

The presence of the Girdle of Venus can work both favorably or negatively, depending on the hand in question. For instance, a hand with a broken Girdle of Venus suggests a nervous disposition or a high-strung personality, while a Girdle that's reinforced by a double or triple line enhances the desire for excitement or fantasies that need constant "refueling." With balancing factors—such as a long, firm thumb; strong major lines that are favorably situated; and firm skin texture—this line adds another dimension to the personality. For example, if a Girdle of Venus is encountered in the Earth hand, its bearer would most likely desire adventure and challenges in their work or life, exhibiting the type of pioneering spirit that belongs to the navigator or explorer.

Now that we've seen the principal factors and emotional similarities that ought to be present for a relationship to be harmonious, the next chapter will fill in the gaps, showing how expectancies in lifestyles and goal orientation figure prominently in partnerships.

+++

CHAPTER 21

Supporting Factors of Compatibility

*A*side from the principal factors on the hand that can predict compatibility, there are some supporting details to observe as well. These are: the zonal balance of the palm, fingers, and thumb; the thumb itself; the skin texture of the hand; the four types of patterns on fingertips; and the shape of fingernails.

The Zonal Balance

As discussed in Chapter 7, the palm is divided into outer- and inner-directed spheres and into active and passive zones that illustrate the interplay of the mental, emotional, and physical aspects of an individual's personality (see Figures 34–36, page 76–80). It's important to notice whether these zones are balanced; if they're not, the analyst needs to establish which of the three spheres are either emphasized or shortchanged. The finger and thumb sections should also be included in this analysis.

It should be evident that someone possessing a hand with a clearly dominant Physical/Instinctual lower zone of the palm probably wouldn't find common ground with a person whose energies are primarily directed into the Mental or Emotional zones.

The Thumb

For the purpose of determining whether the thumbs of two individuals are compatible, I'd like to reiterate the main characteristics of this digit (discussed in detail in Chapter 4).

- A long thumb is reflective of an individual's staying power.

- A shorter-than-average thumb is a regressive sign—which isn't to say that such a person couldn't be successful, but they'll have to work hard for it.

- A thick thumb indicates determination, which may border on obstinacy, especially if the joints are stiff and inflexible. If the base section is set firmly, but the nail section is flexible and bends easily, such a person tends to be receptive toward the opinions of others.

- A slender thumb, especially if it's very flexible, describes a person who desires to "go with the flow." If the base section is firmly rooted and offers resistance when pressure is applied, this indicates that the individual has a will of their own, which acts as a good balance for this type of thumb.

- A "wasted" thumb has a slender second phalange, which is indicative of tact and discriminating taste.

- The "arched" thumb reveals versatility, as well as a tendency toward extravagance (the "stubborn ledge" points to the same trait).

- People with the bulbous formation referred to as the "murderer's thumb" tend to exhibit an explosive or brutal temper.

- The nail or top section of the thumb reflects the will of a person, while the second phalange measures their logic or reasoning power. The two sections should be balanced; a very long first section would most likely belong to someone with a strong will who doesn't use their powers of deduction—but a much longer second section reflects indecision. Such a person might have problems making up their mind, which could result in missed opportunities.

As you can see, people's differences and similarities can become quite apparent from comparing their thumbs.

Skin Texture

Whether a person has thick, medium/elastic, or paper-thin skin can best be determined by touch. As mentioned previously, the texture of one's skin is a genetic characteristic rather than the result of one's occupation. A manual laborer may get tough, callused skin, but their skin ridges are the same as they were at birth.

Naturally, coarse or leathery skin is better equipped to handle heavy, rough materials—and course skin texture often goes together with a matching temperament, as these people aren't known to possess either a sensitive or fussy nature (which is a hallmark of thin-skinned people). It should be obvious that two people with such diverse skin textures would find themselves at odds in their preferences of work, interests, or lifestyles. Just imagine two people with such opposite skin textures going on a camping trip together! The one with thick skin would most probably enjoy "roughing it" and wouldn't mind the primitive conditions or the flies in the tent, while the thin-skinned person would hate being without their creature comforts. Conversely, the thin-skinned type would be in their element at parties or social functions, while their thick-skinned partner would most likely be utterly bored and be itching to get away.

Patterns on Fingertips

To summarize briefly, there are physical, as well as psychological, characteristics associated with these patterns. For instance, the Arch is the simplest of all the patterns, and is most often seen in Elementary or Practical hands;

it points to strong emotional attachment toward family and traditions. The Loop pattern is associated with versatility and the ability to adjust to life's situations. However, if Loops are found on all digits, this characteristic may be taken to extremes, showing a lack of stability or determination. The Whorl pattern is a sign of individuality, and is associated with a driving force that's identified with the masculine side of a personality, showing a desire for activity and leadership. Too many Whorls would show an overabundance of these characteristics. The Tented Arch pattern is a sign of a high degree of idealism, which can work both positively or negatively—when these people's expectations aren't met, they would tend to be very disappointed or disillusioned. Similar to those with the Whorl, people possessing Tented Arches are known for their individuality.

Shapes of Fingernails

The shapes of a person's fingernails also give many clues to their inherent temperament. In Chapter 5, I illustrated the different shapes of nails, which are briefly summarized below.

- Shorter-than-average nails reflect a personality that's full of "vim and vigor." People with such nails are quick-witted . . . and quite often have a temper to match. They have a tendency to be critical of others and themselves. Short-nailed individuals are the "doers" of the world, not the "dreamers."

- When the nails are broader than they are long, tension and frustration (which is often brought on by themselves) is increased. Thanks to their inner stress, these people are predisposed to be nail-biters and also tend to develop ulcers. Such nails are likely to be encountered among the Spatulate and Square types, rather than the Philosophic, Conic/Artistic, or Sensitive/Intuitive categories.

- If the nails are extremely short and small, the individual has a miserly nature, to say the least, which will be reflected in their narrow lifestyle. If such nails are found on square-tipped fingers, it points to the person leading a dull and unadventurous life.

- Nails that are about as broad as they are long generally belong to honest, dependable, practical, and resourceful personalities. Due to their inborn sense of loyalty, they make excellent friends. Nails of this shape may be seen among many hand types, but are rarely encountered on long, tapering fingers.

- Dish-shaped nails are not a sign of robust health. They may have taken on this shape after having experienced trauma, or it may be the result of continual tension or stress.

- People with long, oval-shaped nails have less vitality than those with broad shapes, but this doesn't imply that they're sickly. It just means that their disposition is more placid, so these individuals tend to conserve their crucial energy. The owners of long, oval-shaped nails are known to have infinite patience with details and people.

- Nails that are very narrow, resembling birds' talons, tend to belong to people who will spot beneficial opportunities with an eagle's eye.

It should be evident that partners possessing similarly shaped nails share many of the attitudes that allow for mutual understanding of each other, but if their nails are of opposite shapes, they should at least be aware of what these differences can signify.

This same awareness can be achieved from all of the factors of compatibility listed above. The principal factors bear greater significance than the supporting factors, but you may find that if the shape of the hand shows compatibility, many of the supporting factors will confirm it.

Here's a fun experiment: Working on a point system, give yourself two points for each of the principal factors of compatibility you share with your partner, and one point for each of the supporting factors. The highest possible score is 13; where you fall with your mate should give you an idea of just how "meant for each other" you actually are.

The next chapters will show the handprints of couples whose relationships have withstood the test of time . . . and others who haven't been so fortunate.

✝ ✝ ✝

CHAPTER 22

Randy and Stephanie—a Good Match

The factors of compatibility are illustrated in the handprints of the couples shown in the following chapters. Unfortunately, some of the supporting factors, such as the shape of fingernails and skin texture, can't be seen from the handprints—these can only be ascertained from an analysis done in person.

Randy, Lawyer
(see Figure 129, page 264)

(see Figure 129, page 264)

- *Primary hand type:* Intellectual/Analytical "Air"

- *Secondary hand type:* Social/Artistic "Fire"

- *Heart line:* Rises high from the Mount of Jupiter

- *Mount of Venus:* Moderate development; circle of Life line is wide but turns inward toward the Mount of Venus at the wrist

- *Zonal distribution:* Shows good balance between the mental, emotional, and physical

- *Thumb:* Average length of thumb; its sections, representing his will and logic, are balanced

Due to Randy's long fingers and the relative square-ness of his palm, his hand falls primarily into the Intellectual category. Yet the rounded fingertips and slanting

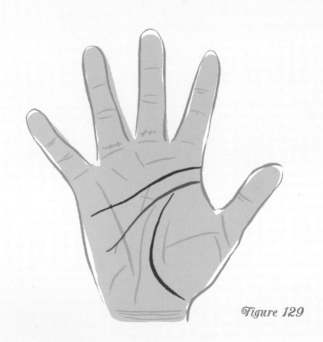

Figure 129

course of the long Head line toward the Mount of Luna show the strong influence of the Artistic/Social personality, combining logic and discerning, analytical thinking with creative imagination and versatility. The influence of the Social/Artistic hand type also reflects Randy's excellent social skills.

The Heart line reveals loyalty in the affections, and the average development of the Mount of Venus suggests vitality and/or empathy. The hand is proportioned nicely and depicts a good zonal balance between physical and mental activities.

The padded Mount of Luna confirms Randy's creative imagination, which is further indicated by the rounded edge of his Percussion. This hand belongs to an excellent "team player" who's equally happy in either a supporting or commanding role. The former is indicated by a Jupiter finger that's somewhat shorter than the Apollo finger, suggesting that Randy's first priority is not a quest for leadership, and that he's genuinely content working at his own speed and on his own projects.

Stephanie, Art Appraiser and Auctioneer
(see Figure 130, page 266)

- *Primary hand type:* Sensitive/Intuitive "Water"

- *Secondary hand types:* Intellectual/Analytical "Air" and Social/Artistic "Fire"

- *Heart line:* Starts from the high point of Mount of Jupiter

- *Mount of Venus:* Plump and widely encircled by the Life line

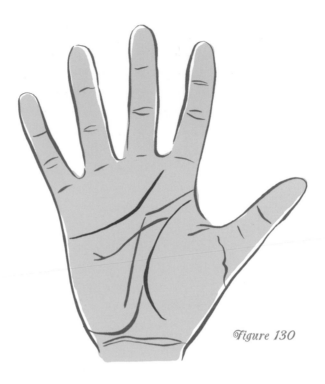

Figure 130

- *Zonal distribution:* Shows good balance between emotional, mental, and physical activities

- *Thumb:* Very long and strong, with a good balance between the first and second sections

The primary type of this beautiful and elegant hand is determined by the oblong shape of the palm and the long, slender fingers—yet two other hand types are also in evidence. Although her primary hand type is Psychic/Intuitive, Stephanie's palm isn't extremely narrow as a pure Water type would be.

An interesting modifying feature in this hand is the presence of a short, straight second Head line, which is situated above the main line. My interpretation of this second line is that Stephanie possesses a practical business sense, which is also confirmed by the small fork that turns upward at the end of her primary Head line. This is referred to as the "Lawyer's Fork," and its presence is associated with business acumen as well as with communication and debating skills. Her ability to be a convincing speaker is further indicated by the long nail phalange of her Mercury finger.

Stephanie's perseverance and staying power are reinforced by her extremely long thumb and its powerful nail section. Her equally lengthy Jupiter finger gives further evidence of her potential and desire for leadership.

Compiling all of the evidence on the hands of this 30-something couple, it seems that they share many factors that point to compatibility and harmony, especially since their hands both show combinations of two types—Intellectual/Analytical (Air) and Social/Dynamic (Fire)—in various degrees. Stephanie's primary hand type, Sensitive/Intuitive (Water), reveals that she can be strongly emotional beneath the surface; this is met and compensated by Randy's understanding and gentle, nonaggressive personality. These two individuals are intellectual and professional equals in their respective fields, and there's no evidence of a power struggle in their private life. This is a good match indeed.

+ + +

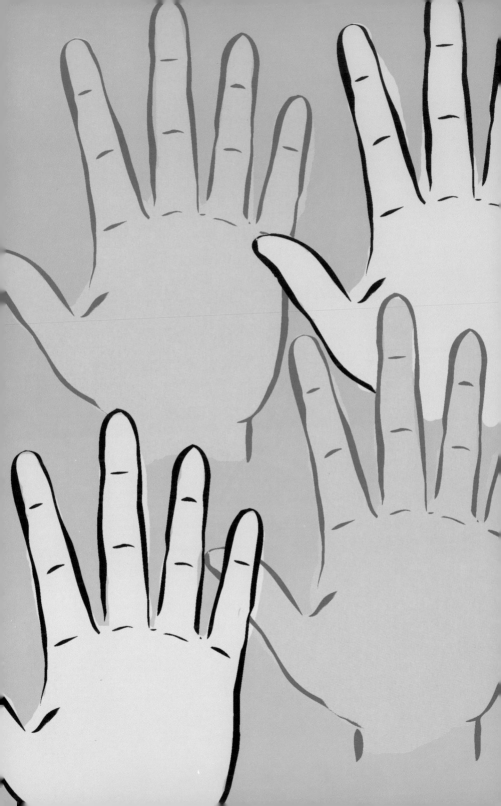

Alice and Bob— Oldies but Goodies

Alice, Handwriting Analyst
(see Figure 131, page 270)

- *Primary hand type:* Social/Dynamic "Fire"

- *Secondary hand types:* Practical/Useful "Earth" and Intellectual/Analytical "Air"

- *Heart line:* Partial Simian formation—that is, the Head and Heart lines are connected by an Influence line

- *Mount of Venus:* Average development

- *Girdle of Venus:* Present, indicating a desire for adventure and variety

- *Zonal distribution:* Good balance of the zones, but the appearance of the partial Simian line and Girdle of Venus point to the need for outer stimuli

- *Thumb:* Long and firm

Although this hand belongs primarily to the Social/Dynamic category, the influence of the practical Earth type is also apparent. The palm, which is only slightly oblong, possesses a sturdiness that's usually absent from the Social/Dynamic hand—this reveals a love of physical activities, and indeed, Alice is an avid sports enthusiast. Even though the fingers are shorter in comparison to the

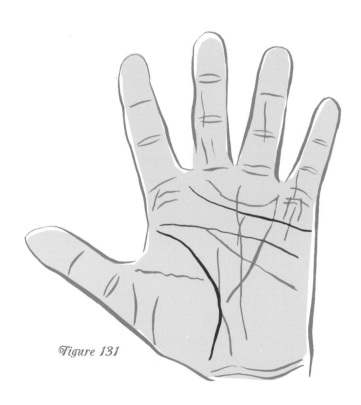

Figure 131

palm, the lengthy, distinctive thumb and long nail sections of the fingers are associated with the Intellectual hand.

The Head line starts apart from the Life line, which points to an independent spirit from an early age—but its fusion with the Heart line in a partial Simian formation on this, her dominant hand (she is left-handed), decreases such favorable characteristics a bit. Yet, as a balancing act, a fork of the Head line toward the Mount of Luna shows Alice's creative imagination and insight, adding another dimension to her personality.

An interesting thing to look at is her Fate (or Career) line, which is enmeshed with the Life line at its beginning point near the wrist. This reveals goals and aspirations starting at an early age, yet the Fate line doesn't continue beyond her 30s, probably due to obligations to or influence from her family.

There's also a vertical line crossing the Simian line and the Girdle of Venus beneath the Apollo finger, which suggests that Alice's attempts at creative endeavors were disappointing or never materialized at all. There are also numerous vertical lines on the Mount of Mercury, which indicate that she has been involved in caregiving situations. Judging from the horizontal bars seen on the Mounts of Mercury and Jupiter, Alice's attempts to realize a fulfilling career may have been thwarted due to her responsibilities to her family.

The Girdle of Venus is placed rather low on her palm, almost as if to replace the Heart line. The length and strength of this marking reveals a restless nature and a very strong desire for variety and stimulation from the outside world. In this hand, the long, distinctive thumb is a very favorable asset, for it lends stability and staying power to her endeavors.

Bob, Computer Scientist
(see Figure 132)

- *Primary hand type:* Analytical/Intellectual "Air"

- *Secondary hand type:* Practical/Useful "Earth"

- *Heart line:* Set low, between the Mounts of Jupiter and Saturn

- *Mount of Venus:* Nicely developed and widely encircled by the Life line

- *Zonal distribution:* Good balance, except for the low-set Heart line—this indicates that emotions may interfere with his reasoning

- *Thumb:* Sturdy, thick thumb of above-average length

Based on the length of fingers and thumb relative to the palm, Bob's primary hand type belongs to the Intellectual/Analytical category. Other characteristics pointing to the Intellectual type are the many additional lines etched into the palmar surface, such as a strongly independent Fate line and the presence of Apollo and Mercury lines—but the influence of the practical, steady Earth hand is very much in evidence as well. In fact, it's interesting to note that, except for the top sections of his fingers and thumb (which show his considerable mental capacity), Bob's hand shape actually resembles the Earth type. This is especially noticeable in his square-tipped fingers and thumb, which reveal his desires to find practical solutions

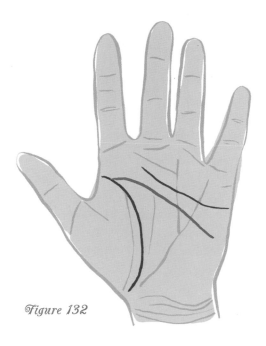

Figure 132

to problems. Bob's love of physical activities is indicated by the fullness of his hand and the development of the Mount of Venus, as well as in the sturdiness of his fingers and thumb.

This couple has withstood the test of time, although I wouldn't give them very high marks in every aspect regarding compatibility. For even though their hands share the combinations of two hand types (Air and Earth) to a certain degree, Alice's primary hand type (Fire) is challenging to Bob's strong secondary type (Earth).

Alice's personality is socially oriented and seeks variety, which is reinforced by her large Girdle of Venus; Bob is home- and hearth-loving, which can be seen in the inward curve of his Life line around the ball of his thumb. Another characteristic of people with this hand type is that they tend to see things in terms of black and white, failing to acknowledge matters that they can't understand or analyze with logic. The result is that such individuals can appear judgmental or obstinate, attitudes that would irk the flexible, versatile Fire type.

Yet, this couple does have much in common—especially in the physical realm, since both enjoy sports activities, together and separately. This is indicated by the firmness of their skin texture and the fullness of their fingers; their robust health and energy is revealed in strong major lines. Bob and Alice, although different in many ways, have enough in common to keep them together for the long haul.

CHAPTER 24

Diane and Andrew—
Disengaged

*T*he handprints shown below belong to a couple who was engaged to be married, but their engagement and relationship have subsequently been terminated. Let's take a look at their hands to see if we can find any clues as to what might have happened.

Diane, Teacher
(see Figure 133, page 276)

- *Primary hand type:* Social/Dynamic "Fire"

- *Secondary type:* Intellectual/Analytical "Air"

- *Heart line:* Rising from the Mount of Jupiter

- *Mount of Venus:* Well developed

- *Zonal distribution:* Good balance, with emphasis on Emotional and Intellectual areas

- *Thumb:* Slender, of average length; moderate angle to palm

Diane's disposition is warm, spontaneous, and emotional, thanks to her Fire type. Her hand has a short inner and a much wider outer Life line, which reflect her two temperaments: Outwardly, she projects an adventurous, fun-loving personality, while her inner Life line reveals

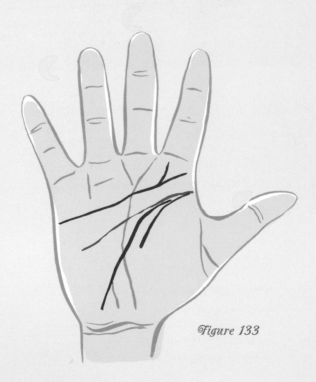

Figure 133

vulnerability that craves the support of those she loves and trusts. This vulnerability is confirmed by her Fate line, which is enmeshed with her Life line, showing close family ties. The Fate line extends upward into her palm far beyond her actual age, with a fork toward the Mount of Jupiter—this signifies strong goals, aspirations, and adaptability.

Diane's Heart line starts from the Mount of Jupiter (with a branch rising to the finger itself), giving a clue to her loyalty in love, as well as her tendency to be overly idealistic; this can result in disappointments when loved ones don't meet her expectations. Obviously, these expectations weren't met in her relationship with Andrew, which may have caused their breakup. Diane needs a warm, loving relationship in which both partners are comfortable and affectionate with each other and are able to verbalize and air their differences in a civilized manner. She also requires a union that would be conducive to cultivating close relationships with family and friends, for this is the kind of environment that Diane would flourish in.

Andrew, Manager
(see Figure 134, page 278)

- *Primary hand type:* Practical/Useful "Earth"

- *Heart line:* Starting point below the Mount of Saturn

- *Mount of Venus:* Extremely distinctive

- *Zonal distribution:* Emphasis on the Physical/Instinctive sphere

- *Thumb:* Strong, thick nail phalange, held at a wide angle to the palm

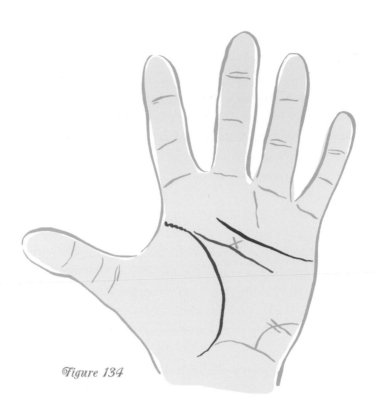

Figure 134

Andrew's square, thick, short-fingered palm displays few lines other than the major ones of Life, Head, and Heart, which is indicative of the Practical personality. His full Mount of Venus reveals a sensuous but self-gratifying nature, which is confirmed by a Heart line that rises from the Mount of Saturn. The Physical/Instinctive sphere dominates this hand, and the presence of a Poison Line—bridging the Mount of Luna with that of Venus—enhances Andrew's tendency to overindulge, be it in the form of food, drink, or sex. This propensity is corroborated by horizontal lines on the Mount of Luna. None of these markings are favorable, especially when coupled with the absence of Fate, Apollo, or Mercury lines, for they would modify and offset the negative aspects to some extent.

This hand isn't without leadership potential—in fact, his full fingers that drift toward Jupiter, as well as his strong thumb that's widely angled from the palm reflect otherwise—but the nature of Andrew's leadership would most likely be by force, displaying little sensitivity toward the needs or concerns of others.

Andrew requires and expects a spouse to fulfill his physical needs; in addition, he doesn't want his partner to demand things he can't provide, such as emotional comfort and sensitivity. Earth types are notorious for being unable to communicate their feelings, and they tend to bottle up their emotions. Although slow to anger, when they do let off steam, it's often destructive and vengeful. I wouldn't be at all surprised if such outbursts contributed to, or were even the cause of, Andrew and Diane's breakup.

Simply by looking at these two handprints, it should be quite obvious that Diane and Andrew's hands belong to diametrically opposite types. This is especially true since they represent almost pure types of Fire and Earth, respectively. In addition, Diane's secondary influence is Air; both Fire and Air are most incompatible with the Earth type . . . which is exactly what Andrew is.

In my opinion, it was very fortunate that Diane and Andrew discovered that their expectations were very different before they married, for this could have resulted in a disastrous union.

Pam and Tony— Who's the Boss?

*T*his couple is in their 40s and has been married for almost 20 years, but is currently undergoing a trial separation. As you'll be able to see from their handprints, they seem to be reasonably well matched, yet perhaps we'll be able to find out why they have opted to separate.

Pam, Real Estate Agent and Homemaker
(see Figure 135, page 282)

- *Primary hand type:* Practical/Useful "Earth"

- *Secondary hand type:* Social/Dynamic "Fire"

CHAPTER 25

- *Heart line:* Rising from the Mount of Jupiter, with a branch toward the Jupiter finger

- *Mount of Venus:* Moderately developed

- *Zonal distribution:* Good balance of the three zones

- *Thumb:* Low-set, average length

This hand belongs almost as much to the Social/ Dynamic category as it does to the Practical Earth type. From the former, it takes the relative squareness of the palm; yet it has rounded edges, which is often found in females of the Practical hand type with the Social/Artistic influence. This is also confirmed by tapering fingers with rounded tips. There are many additional lines etched

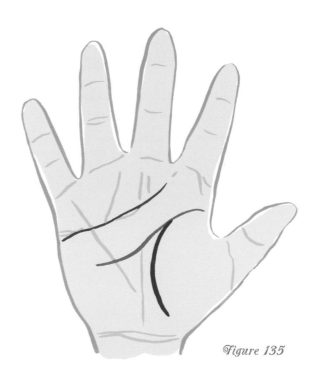

Figure 135

into the palmar surface, and the Head line curves slightly toward the Mount of Luna, again displaying the presence of the Social/Artistic type.

Tony, Insurance Company Owner
(see *Figure 136*)

- *Primary hand type:* Intellectual/Analytical "Air"

- *Heart line:* Rising from between the Mounts of Jupiter and Saturn

- *Mount of Venus:* Firm and fleshy

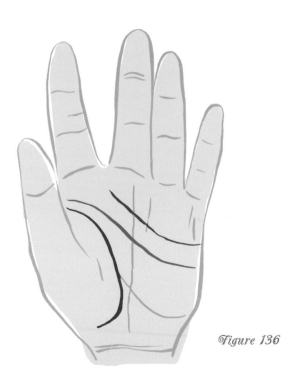

Figure 136

- *Zonal distribution:* Good balance in all three zones

- *Thumb:* Extremely long and powerful

This hand conveys power and energy, seen in the clearly marked major lines and the mounts. The Mounts of Jupiter, Upper and Lower Mars, Venus, and Luna are especially distinctive. The Percussion reveals resourcefulness and ingenuity; and the long, independent course of the Head line attests to a very keen intellectual, analytical, and creative mind.

What surfaces from these two handprints is an imbalance of power. Pam's rounded palm and fingertips belong to a congenial, warm, and loving personality. Although her Mercury finger is longer than average, which reveals good communication skills, it's set low, reflecting a lack of confidence. The Jupiter finger is shorter than Apollo, suggesting that she "takes a back seat" and tends to compromise too much. The strong Fate line, starting from the wrist, reveals independence from an early age on, but the line stops before meeting the Head line at the approximate age of 28, which suggests that there were no ongoing career goals from that time on.

Tony's Fate line, on the other hand, forges ahead toward its destination point, the Mount of Saturn, which indicates that his goals are progressive and reach far ahead of his actual age. His powerful and exceptionally long Jupiter finger (which is positioned independently), together with such a powerful and lengthy thumb, points to someone who is used to take charge of things. While the positioning of his Jupiter finger reflects a "go-getter" personality, the closely aligned thumb and clinging fingers of Apollo and Saturn exhibit a measure of caution.

I believe that Pam's innate desire for independence and her ability to manage her own life will surface again, now that she's forced into this trial separation. If this couple should reconcile, it won't just be on Tony's terms—Pam will have relearned to stand on her own feet, and it will indeed become an equal *partnership.*

After weighing the factors that show compatibility (or a lack of it) in the hands of potential partners, it should make people at least aware of the differences *and* the similarities they have with their significant others. This should subsequently help them decide whether or not a relationship would be beneficial for both of them.

Afterword

*N*ow that my book has come to an end, I'd like to say a few last words to you, the reader. I sincerely hope that *In the Palm of Your Hand* has given you an awareness of hands that you never had before.

How should you start reading hands? My suggestion is to begin with your own. Try to be as objective as you possibly can in seeing not only the positive signs, but also the less favorable ones as well. Don't be alarmed by these, because every human being has both strong and weak traits. By observing your own hands, you'll be able to judge whether the signs that are indicated are correct. Then, proceed by asking family members and friends if they'd like to receive a hand reading. In my experience, they'll be delighted to say yes and will often gladly tell you whether your evaluation is accurate or not.

You'll also find that there are many signs or lines in the hands that aren't mentioned in my book, or in any other book on palmistry, for that matter. You may then come to realize just how unique each hand is; it's up to you to be the judge and interpreter. In order to do so, you should first gather all of the information pertaining to the physical aspect of the hand. Next, observe the major lines and their positioning, as well as any additional lines and markings. After all of the available data is collected and recorded, you should then form a composite picture of the hand to discover the quantity and quality of the creative and/or destructive forces revealed within the hand. I feel that the ability to poll all known facts, and then to add the "unknown or untried" to it, is the mark of an excellent, insightful hand reader.

Good luck!

Bibliography and Resource List

Altman, Nathaniel, *Die Praxis Des Handlesens (The Practice of Hand Reading)*. Knaur Publishing, 1987.

Biccum, Gerry E., *Handology*. Beyond Words Publishing, Inc., 1989.

Brandon-Jones, David, *Practical Palmistry*. South Asia Books, 1994.

Broekman, Marcel, *The Complete Encyclopedia of Practical Palmistry*. Prentice Hall, 1972.

Brenner, Elizabeth, *Hand in Hand*. Celestial Arts, 1981.

Cheiro, *Language of the Hand*. ARC Books, 1968 (34th printing).

———, *Cheiro's Complete Palmistry*. University Books, 1969.

de Saint-Germain, Compte C., *The Practice of Palmistry for Professional Purposes*. Newcastle Publishing Co., 1973.

Gerstein, Liz, *Handwriting & Palmistry*. Nouvelle Press, 1994.

Gettings, Fred, *The Book of the Hand*. Hamlyn Publishing Co., 1960.

————, *The Book of Palmistry*. Triune Books, 1974.

————, *Palmistry Made Easy*. Wilshire Books, 1966.

Hipskind, Judith, *Palmistry: The Whole View*. Llewellyn Publishing, 1977.

Hutchinson, Beryl, *Your Life in Your Hands*. Sphere Books Ltd., 1977.

Jaquin, Noel, *Scientific Palmistry*. George H. Doran Co., 1934.

Luxon, Bettina, *Your Hand in Business*. Rosters Ltd., 1988.

Meier, Nellie Simmons, *Lion's Paws*. Barrows, Mussey Publishing, 1937.

Niblo, *The Complete Palmist*. Originally published in 1900. Republished by Newcastle Publishing Co., Inc., 1982.

Ohashi, *Reading the Body: Ohashi's Book of Oriental Diagnosis*. Aquarian Press, 1992.

Oxenford, Ina, *Life Studies in Palmistry*. Upcott Gill, 1899. Republished by S.R. Publishers and Scolar Press Ltd., 1971.

Sheridan, Jo, *What Your Hand Reveals*. Bell Publishing Co.

Squire, Elizabeth Daniels, *Fortune in Your Hands*. Fleet Publishing, 1960.

Wolff, Dr. Charlotte, *The Human Hand*. Meethuen & Co., 1942.

————, *Studies in Hand-Reading*. Alfred A. Knopf, 1938.

Glossary

Apollo Finger: Ring finger. Symbolizes beauty and artistic expression. Also stands for intimate commitments; bearer of wedding/engagement ring. *Line:* Below the Apollo finger, enhancing the above qualities. *Mount:* Elevation below Apollo finger that also enhances these characteristics.

Bracelets: Horizontal lines at the wrist; usually three in number. If clearly defined, they suggest good health.

Cheiro: Famous 19th-century palmist, author, and lecturer.

Fate Line:	Also called the "Line of Destiny," "Career line" or "Effort line." Usually found in the center of the palm, starting from the wrist and ending on or near the Mount of Saturn. May have other starting points in the palm. This line is not present in all hands. Although not a major line, it is very significant, for it reveals goal orientation and adaptability.
Girdle of Venus:	A semicircular line that lies below the Jupiter, Saturn, and Apollo fingers. Signifies a desire for romance, a craving for outer stimuli, and a restless nature. Not present in all hands.
Head Line:	Also called the "Line of Mentality." It is a major line and indicates mental capacity and concentration.
Heart Line:	This is a major line and measures the quality of the heart as an organ. The direction of this line reveals the type of our affections.
Influence Line:	A line connecting two lines, such as Heart and Head, Fate and Life, and so on. Also, an Influence line may connect the two ends of a broken or interrupted line, showing that problems or obstacles have been overcome.
Intuition Crescent:	A semicircular line found at the outer edge of the palm near the Mount of Luna. Shows intuition and a sixth sense.
Jupiter Finger:	The index finger. Relates to leadership abilities and how a person handles their responsibilities. *Mount:* Elevation below this finger. If distinctive, the qualities of the Jupiter finger are enhanced.
Lawyer's Fork:	Fork in the Head line in the direction of Mercury. Shows good communication skills and an aptitude for business.

Life Line: This is a major line and is often considered the most important one. Encircles the ball of the thumb (the Mount of Venus).

Luna, Mount: This mount lies in the lower part of the hand near the outer edge of the palm, in the Instinctive sphere. If it's well developed, it reveals creative imagination.

Major Lines: They consist of Life, Head, and Heart lines. The latter two may be fused together, which is called the "Simian Line." See also *Simian Line*.

Marriage Lines: Horizontal lines below the Mercury finger. Also referred to as "Relationship Lines." Signifies a desire to enter intimate relationships and commitments.

Mars, Mounts: There are two mounts: (1) The Lower Mars, situated at the insertion of the thumb, symbolizes a fighting spirit and courage; and (2) the Upper Mars, situated at the outer edge of the palm below the little finger, symbolizes endurance and persistence.

Mercury Finger: This is the little finger, symbolizing the art and skill of communication in all fields. It is also referred to as the "Finger of Enterprise." *Mount:* The elevation below this finger. If prominent, it enhances the qualities of the Mercury finger.

Mounts: These are the eight elevations on the palmar surface. They are: Venus, Luna, Upper and Lower Mars, Jupiter, Saturn, Apollo, and Mercury.

Mystic Cross: This is a cross found primarily in the center of the palm between the Head and Heart lines. It indicates interest in mysticism and the occult.

Percussion: Outer edge of the palm. If rounded, it is a sign of resourcefulness and ingenuity.

Phalanges: This is the name for the sections in fingers and thumb—that is, the *nail, middle,* or *base* phalange.

Saturn Finger: The middle finger. Symbolizes home, stability, and fairness, and the acceptance of law and order. *Mount:* Elevation below this finger. If distinctive, it enhances the qualities of the Saturn finger; if overdeveloped, it shows a morbid personality; if flat, it reveals disappointments.

Simian Line: The fusion of the Head and Heart lines. May indicate lack of objectivity.

Sister line: A line accompanying a major line, or the Fate, Apollo, and Mercury lines. Since it strengthens the respective main lines, it's considered to be favorable.

Venus, Mount: The root or ball of the thumb. If pronounced, it enhances vitality, desire for physical/sexual activities, and empathy.

Via Lasciva: Also referred to as the "Poison line." Situated near the Mount of Luna; often connects the Mounts of Luna and Venus. Indicates a proclivity toward allergies or excesses in food, drink, sex, drugs, or alcohol.

Writer's Fork: A fork in the Head line toward the Mount of Luna; reveals an aptitude for writing.

About the Author

Liz Gerstein came to the United States in 1958 from her native Switzerland. Although she made her living as a professional interpreter and translator, she has had a life-long interest in graphology. In the United States, she continued and broadened her studies of handwriting analysis and decided to make graphology her second career. As a certified handwriting analyst, she believes in the *holistic* approach to unblocking the complexity of human nature and behavior, and she has gravitated toward other related parasciences, such as palmistry, in trying to discover a person's *modus operandi*. She has successfully demonstrated her innovative method of interrelating *graphology* and *hand-ology* in her book, *Handwriting and Palmistry—Discover Personality and Potential from Handwriting and Hands*, published in 1994. Liz teaches privately and at the Society of Handwriting Analysts of the Greater Washington area; and is also a guest lecturer on *Cunard, Celebrity,* and *Costa* cruise ships.

We hope you enjoyed this Hay House Lifestyles book.
If you would like to receive a free catalog
featuring additional Hay House books and products,
or if you would like information about the
Hay Foundation, please contact:

Hay House, Inc.
P.O. Box 5100
Carlsbad, CA 92018-5100

(760) 431-7695 or **(800) 654-5126**
(760) 431-6948 (fax) or **(800) 650-5115 (fax)**

Hay House Australia Pty Ltd
P.O. Box 515
Brighton-Le-Sands NSW 2216
phone: 1800 023 516
e-mail: info@hayhouse.com.au

Please visit the Hay House Website at: **hayhouse.com**